1 Hot Mom Productions

I'M-POSSIBLE!

DAILY
Minutes of Motivation

31 days of daily inspiration, transforming the TOTAL you through spiritual, physical, and life applications.

ABOUT THE AUTHOR

Stacie McCall Harris is known for her big hair and her big personality. You will feel her infectious personality through her story telling. She is a firm believer in being contagious in a good way and that there is no such thing as impossible, but there is such a thing as I'M-POSSIBLE. As an only child who grew up with her parents as her life coaches, Stacie was an undersized, over-achiever that would work her way to becoming an honor- student, and stand out three–sport athlete in high school. After deciding to play basketball for the first time in 4th grade, she received the guidance and support system from her parents. Through their support, her hard work, commitment, and discipline, she received a full basketball scholarship to the University of Michigan being the shortest player at 5'3 in the dynamic Big Ten Conference during her tenure.

While at Michigan, she received her degree in Public Relations/Communications. Her character and work ethic proved to be a lifestyle as she was awarded "The Henry & Nancy Newlin Award" honoring the school's top three athletes. Stacie's consistency and ability to focus led to being on Michigan's top 10 list for having a 93% Free Throw Average during her Senior year in which she was named Co-Captain.

After college, Stacie's walk in life guided her toward health and fitness. Always adept in developing a plan and working diligently with her whole person, she enjoyed a beautiful season in her life through success in fitness competitions and motherhood. Stacie shared her knowledge and passion for life and inspired others through personal training and fitness for the next few years.

Life as a young mother proved to be challenging yet exciting with a whirlwind of opportunities all at the same time. With a plan and work to do, Stacie found herself living in Los Angeles… literally living the dream of millions and managing her son, CJ Sanders, who became a well known actor in the movie "Ray" starring Jamie Foxx as the Young Ray Charles.

Currently married to 12 Year NFL Veteran and Super Bowl Champion Corey Harris, Stacie is a busy Sports Mom orchestrating the lives of her family. Her work ethic has again shown proof positive as she continues the diligent development of her former Hollywood child star, now All-

American athlete son CJ, along with guiding her two daughters Cierra Sanders, and Cori Harris into their purpose. She is excited for you to journey with her in this book as you take daily measures of finding your own life's purpose.

Dedication

This book is dedicated to my parents who are two of my best friends: **William H. McCall Jr.** and **Patricia McCall-Steele**. I am forever grateful for God choosing you to be my parents and to be the ones who guided me on my life's journey. Your love, commitment, hard work, and sacrifices have allowed me to become the woman I am today. Many thought the work was tough but we always knew we were a "team". We got the job done! To my step- father **Raymond Steele**, thank you for being there for my mother and for always being so understanding and helpful. To my step-mom **Liz Taylor,** thank you for always staying connected.

I also dedicate this book to my loving husband, **Corey Harris**. Thank you for always believing in me and helping each and every one of my dreams, goals, and passions come to life whenever and however I needed you. It has not been an easy journey, but it is "ours" that we own, cherish, and will always pound the pavement "together". I look forward to completing this love journey that God has blessed us to share together.

Last but not least, I dedicate this book to my children **CJ and Cierra Sanders, Cori, and Lauren Harris**. I am so blessed to be your mother. Words can't express the joy you bring to me. Thank you for trusting me to guide you on this extraordinary life journey that God has specifically designed for you. We have accomplished so much together and to think there is so much more ahead is amazing! Always keep God first, and live every day on purpose with passion. I love my Harris/Sanders Huddle.

Special recognition to **Coach Pat Parker**, for being my very first basketball coach and helping me believe that I was capable of leading a team. R.I.P, Coach; you started the point guard in me!

Special recognition to my Grandmother **Edith McCall,** I often think of you. There is so much I wish that we could share. I know you would be so proud. Thank you for the wonderful memories. I still eat Donatos Pizza the way we always liked to share together. This is for you!

Acknowledgments

God: you are so worthy and awesome! I praise you and thank you daily for calling me forth to represent the kingdom in my talents, gifts, and with my family. Thank you for the whispers, the shakings, the trials, the triumphs, and the people you have surrounded my life with to equip me to be the woman I am today. I am grateful you spoke through my life to give me this book to share and bless so many others in calling out the purposed life you have for them.

The Harris family, my father and mother in law George Harris and Ida Mae Harris, for welcoming us into the family with such love. To my brothers and sisters in law, Donald, George, and Roc Harris, Cheryl Satterfield, and Natalie Moss for being the brothers and sisters I never had.

Special thanks to Marcus & Tina Wilson and Kelvin & Donna Jones for the many nights you have kept CoCo so I could have quality time to spend with my husband and to write in peace. To Terry and Penny Kennedy: thank you for listening to me talk about this book during our work out sessions and believing and reminding me it would be worth it and a huge success. Thank you to my Aunt Ada Cummings who always keeps CoCo styling, and for all the love.

Thank you to my former coaches, at every level, that saw something in me before I even saw it in me. Your wisdom and guidance helped to mold me into the tenacious competitor that I am today. You challenged me to be a leader and allowed me to see I could be a contender at anything I wanted to be. A special thank you to my friend, and former first teammate, Christa Parker, She asked me to join the basketball team, because they needed a point guard. It all started there and blossomed.

Much love to my BFF Twyla Dillard from grade school, we have always stayed connected through the years. Thank you for always coming to see me when I am home and getting me out of the house! LaTara Jones, thank you for being my recruit and saying yes to "Michigan". Now, we are connected forever! Love you always.

To all of my former basketball teammates at every level: without you, there would be no me. You trusted me as your captain and point guard and always had my back. My track girls sweat blood! Yep! We ran them down and made a household name from Christ the King to Bishop Hartley! We were the record setters for sure! My 4x800 relay girls, Shannon, Stephanie, and Courtney… thank you for the encouragement and the love during the State meet. Today, I know my strength and the importance of team because of you!

To my Next level team: I'M-POSSIBLE! Thank you to my friend and business partner Raiko

Dai. We have talked about next level living and all of the goals we wanted to obtain. This book has been ready to be birthed for two years and you stuck by my side. Thank you for your friendship, encouragement, talks, and awesome web designs for all of my businesses. Wayne Mitchell: thank you for my logo design and bringing my creative mind to life in such a beautiful way. Your patience and belief in me is a true blessing. To Bev Moser, my photographer, who waited all day and was willing to do a late night shoot: thank you! You are the best and that is why I use you for every photo shoot!

To Stacy Black, my longtime stylist and friend: your talks, personal shopping, advice, and styling have always had me fabulous, and a trendsetter for years! You, my friend, are so professional and talented and your time is coming to show the world! To Krystal Berry: you are the most patient and diligent editor I know. Thank you for your kind words and seeing me through this project step-by-step.

To Wallace King: YES! We did that! You are specific and so gifted! I love that. I made you WORK baby, but it was WORTH it! Thank you for bringing my vision to life! To Tenesia Crook, my long time friend and former relay mate, thank you for your inspiration and providing a meal plan to jump start me and get me right for my pictures! My awesome, talented, and handsome trainer Lester Blanton: thank you for kicking my butt… in a good way. You pushed me physically beyond where I believed I could go! Your encouragement and little brother talks helped mentally prepare me for my next chapter.

CJ Sanders: son, thank you for your kind words. You are truly my inspiration and your encouragement and faith in me, as your mother, makes all the hard work and sacrifices more than worth it! To Tracie Bonds and Mechelle McNair: thank you for being my long and dear friends that have seen me evolve over the years. Thank you for believing in me and wanting to bless me with being a special part of this book. A special thank you to my dear friend Sonia Everett McKie who walked this walk before me and helped guide me through the process to avoid costly errors. The late night talks, and pushes to continue on were so encouraging. To my nephew Demetrius Harris: thank you for your advice and introductions to help guide me through this tedious process of bringing my first book to life.

For everyone who 'stood in the gap'… prayed for and encouraged me: I thank you! I am so grateful to my many friends and family who have all been there at particular seasons in my life and who know me as "Stacie McCall…" where it all began. Because of all of you, what I thought might not ever be possible has become I'M-POSSBIBLE! GOD BLESS EACH AND EVERY ONE OF YOU!

Introduction

It's time to take charge of your life and turn "Impossible" to: I'M-POSSIBLE!

Most of us are familiar with the cliché, "I got out on the wrong side of the bed this morning," which has consistently been used as a way of explaining our bad attitude or defining the outcome of having a bad day. The one thing that rings true is that your outcome can truly be manifested by how you mentally start your day.

'1 Hot Mom's' daily minutes of motivation will help you begin with an understanding of what God says about you and the purpose He has for your life. This book seeks to take you through my personal journey, while helping you reflect on your own divine journey…a way of applying life principles to create a new and more empowered way of thinking. With this 31-day devotion, you will learn how to equip yourself to take control of your life instead of letting it take control of you. Each day will also include a fitness tip on how to become consistent in your health endeavors by making it a lifestyle. You can have the day and the life that you deserve. No more just existing, being complacent, and making it through, but be consistent in how you start and this will give you the results you are looking for.

It is time to be consistent and to stop delaying who you know you were created to be!

How much longer will you settle for less? What does being your best and living in your dream look like? If you are not sure, it is time to discover and live life on purpose! Are you up for the Challenge? Yes you are! Begin today by stretching yourself to new heights with I'M-POSSIBLE to help shift and transform the TOTAL you by living your best life yet! I challenge you to dig in and discover the possibilities! It is time to change what seemed impossible to finding the "I'M-POSSIBLE" in you!

"It's not where you've been that will determine your outcome; it is what you believe and where see yourself going."

What do you believe? Who has God created you to be? What are you doing with it and who is going with you? Just take a moment to answer each of these questions. Initially reading over the questions, it sounds fairly simple… until you really stop and realize you can't answer all of the questions confidently. What does having true understanding and beliefs that you were created to do great things feel like? What is it that you are hoping for? Was there something that caused you to want to read more about this? Whatever it may be, you realize that there is a gap between where you currently are and where you want to be.

"For I know the plans I have for you," declares the Lord, "plans to prosper you and not to harm you, plans to give you a hope and a future."

-Jeremiah 29:11 (NIV)

When we go back to what was spoken over us, before we were ever born, and read what God's purpose is for our lives, it should take a little pressure off of us... knowing the plan has already been written. It is our road map to where we are going and our playbook for winning. You were blessed way before you were ever cursed. Whatever doubt has crept in because of experiences in your past, you should never completely wash away what has been spoken about your future. It all comes down to: making an instant decision in who you will believe, understanding the power of who created you, and knowing that your life, from your very first breath, was designed for a specific purpose.

Usually, your purposes are not one specific thing as we are often searching for and fall short of discovering. A part of purpose is serving and enjoyment of it. So if you are serving and enjoying it, you are fulfilling a purpose. If you are trying to figure out the one thing that will be the "cure all" for discovering true happiness, you will always be in search of that. God didn't just give you a gift or a talent, but He gives in multiples. He has equipped us with gifts to be expressed through using our talents. Know that you are NOT one-dimensional.

How often have you wanted something so bad, but when you got it, you found out that it didn't bring you the real joy or sense of accomplishment that you thought it would? The joy is in learning during the process and not just rushing to get to the final destination. The process is where we are shaped and molded so that when we arrive, it is really just the icing on the cake. For example: when we get a promotion, receive a good report, or win a championship, we bask in the moment because of how it feels... not the actual goal reached. We enjoy the feeling of accomplishment and not just the accomplishment itself. This book seeks to help you discover your everyday purpose which will bring about that accomplished "feeling". With this, in every day and in every situation, focus first on the hope...knowing that God is shaping your future, and equipping you to help you prosper. Now knowing this, doesn't that make you feel good?

This book was put on my heart because at some point, I too could not answer all the questions at certain times in my life. I understand the frustration of going through the motions or feeling like there is more to life than where you are presently. You beat yourself up over past opportunities that you think you have missed and possibly may not get anymore. So, your mind is locked in a time warp… not allowing you to move forward. Consider a missed opportunity or past failure a lesson learned which, was a time of necessary growth. Take your mind off of the "what if" and be thankful for the "I know now!"

I truly understand that God gives us multiple situations to discover a piece of ourselves which will ultimately add up to our whole being and take us on the correct journey of walking in our destiny of true happiness. Look at your journey as walking on the path and picking up clues of discovery along the way. Each one that you apply, whether it is good or bad, takes you further on the path to the next clue. It is the knowledge given along the way that will help "stretch" you. Be thankful of ALL the knowledge you have acquired in your "life" journey. Decide today that if you fail at something, fail forward and if you fall, look up so that you know you can only go up! So, get up! Take a positive outlook and life will no longer consume you negatively. Just keep walking on the path and looking for the next clue… keeping your eyes forward and your feet planted …being expectant of a hope and a future.

Think of someone that always seems to have a smile on their face and is "Happy-go-lucky". That is a choice they made and they are conditioning themselves to receive positive things in return. Put on your armor of happiness and shine instead of hiding in the darkness and laying low in the valley. It is truly time to shout from the mountaintop, because that is what you were crafted to do!

> *"I will praise you, for I am fearfully and wonderfully made; marvelous are your works, and my soul knows very well."*
>
> *-Psalm 139:14 (NIV)*

I have learned to stop searching for that one thing that will be the "tell all "to who I am and what I was created to do. Now, I look to prosper in the place that God has me in at that time, and grow as a person from each of them. Now, we can better understand the question, "who are you taking with you?" In living out your dream, which is the goal and desire of most, it should never just have you in it. In every gift, opportunity given, and in every blessing bestowed upon you, it is never just about YOU. Someone could be in the same situation as you have and you can be the one to confirm an answer or help guide them in the right direction. Guess what? You just dropped a clue on their path! The future is in knowing you can be of service in every area of your life to someone else. Your life has meaning and a purpose, and God is using you to be a difference maker. In that alone is who you were created to be and the hope in knowing your life is really much more than just what is in it for you. God has and wants a promising future for you.

"Trust in the Lord with all your heart, and lean not on your own understanding; in all your ways submit to him, and he will make your paths straight."

-Proverbs 3:5-6 (NIV)

This book is meant, firstly, to jump start you into consistency; this is the main ingredient to accomplishment. If you can be consistent in something, then you will not be content with mediocrity. It is important that the first thing you do is prepare your mind and your spirit which set the course for the rest of your day. Putting on your shield and armor of protection of God's words will cover you for the day.

I thought of the title *I'M-POSSIBLE* because so often, as women, we look at the impossible. We look at the negative before choosing to focus on the positive. It is time to realize that everything about you is possible as you get to know who you are and what you want out of life. It is time to take the time to get to know you and all of you better. Take time to love, each and every day, the person you look at in the mirror... through the flaws and the perfections.

This is what this book will give you: a new sense of reflection on becoming the complete you, and a realization that all of who you ever wanted to be is certainly within you. It gives you a plan to follow while expanding your growth and creativity. I might give you the guidelines, but I want you to bring your own uniqueness to help get the task done! Don't be afraid to do you and be YOU. You are original and authentic and in every area of your life, you should feel confident in being just that: JUST YOU.

The devotions start with filling your spirit, first, with the promises and the word of God. When you 'fill yourself up,' it is easier to pour into others when you are not on empty. Start your tank on full to maneuver more smoothly through the chaos that we know will filter your day. Allow his word to relate to your daily life with a plan of action to be able to go out and know there is a purpose for that day. It is not that you won't experience trials or hard times, but it does not have to be a BAD DAY. It is important to transition from a bad day to a bad moment.

You can determine your outcome by transforming your thinking. I will help you condition yourself for that. Literally, take a moment and then move on… no more consuming and altering the entire day and path that you are meant to be on. *I'm-Possible* will help you to see that mistakes and mishaps, from your past, were not made to keep you stuck, but to spring you forward. Every lemon can be made into lemonade, and every misfortune can be made to be "I am fortunate." It is all a matter of perception and choice. So always choose the better.

In transforming the mind, I also find it important to transform the body at the SAME TIME. Your mind and your body are connected, so why wait to better one and not the other. At the end of each daily motivation, I will give you fitness tips to help get you started with an effective yet easy way to look at fitness as a lifestyle. You don't want to have a strong mind and a weak body or vice-versa.

Getting Started:

"Commit to the Lord whatever you do, and He will establish your plans."

-Proverbs 16:3 (NIV)

Before diving into your first day, I want you to complete a few exercises that will help you have a clear focus on where you are and what you want to accomplish by the time you finish this book. Print out the following questions with your answers and post them up where you can see them daily. At the end of the book, you will go through them again to see what has changed. If you can't answer them, it is okay. You should still print out the questions because by the end of the book, you will be able to answer those questions and some of your previous answers may have changed or have information that needs to be added to it.

Write down the answers, that first come to your mind, in your *1 Hot Mom* Journal. There is no need to make it a task; just use it as your starting point. It is important to write down your thoughts as they come to you. Having one place where you record your notes and thoughts, helps to keep you from being scattered. Call it your 'Faith Filled" journal where you record all of the promises and blessings of God that you can refer to as a refueling of the spirit.

Life Application:

- When you close your eyes and see yourself living out your dream, what does she look like and what is she doing?
- How do you feel? Is she happy?
- When are you your happiest? What does being your happiest feel like? What else can you accomplish when you are feeling this way?
- What 5 main goals do you want to accomplish, and what is each time line? Why is each one important to you?
- What are your current health and fitness levels? Are you happy where you are?
- Sum up your life in one sentence. What do you want people to say and remember about you when you are gone?
- Select a scripture that best defines where you are and what you struggle with the most. Apply this, daily, to your life before you say or do anything else. *Ex. If you are struggling with fear or doubt the following scripture can help you in this area as you speak it over your life:*

"Even though I walk through the darkest valley, I will fear no evil, for you are with me; your rod and your staff, they comfort me."

-Psalm 23:4 (NIV)

Fitness Application:

- Get a fitness journal that you will use for the completion of your 31 days. Write down the answers below so that you can refer to them later.
- What are your fitness goals?
- What have you done in the past and were not successful in sticking to so that you could reach your goals?
- Take measurements of your arms, legs, and stomach.
- I am not a big fan of getting on the scale, but I want you to get on the scale today and not again until you have completed the 31 days; inches matter more than weight loss!
- Write down in your journal that you will stick and stay the course of your fitness plan throughout the 31 days. It takes 21 days to create a habit, so with an extra ten days, you will be well on your way.

DAY 1:

"Suit Up and Get in the Game"

"Therefore put on the full armor of God, so that when the day of evil comes, you may be able to stand your ground, and after you have done everything, to stand."

-Ephesians 6:13 (NIV)

Good morning ladies! You should be excited! You have decided that enough was enough and today, you are going to make a change and do something different. No more insanity: doing the same thing and expecting different results. No more thinking about it and simply watching others be about it. Winning in the life you are meant to have means that you can't be a spectator. You have to put on your gear, lace up your shoes, and get in the game to be a part of the action.

Every day you have to imagine putting on your armor and shielding yourself before you walk out the door. Spin around, put on your cape, and your crown like wonder woman. When you know you are protected, you can go into battle with confidence. Once you walk out the door, you know the battle will begin in some capacity, but there is no feeling like knowing you have on your shield of protection. You are ready to fight the good fight and your job is to approach your goal, and not get distracted, misguided, or left behind. Confidently, go out and take control of your life today.

First, you must fill your spirit with the word of God knowing he has a hope and a future already lined up for you. Each day, your steps are ordained to walk towards your destiny. If you are not protected, you can get injured in a way that will set you back for a while. It's similar to a boxer letting his guard down even for a minute and the opponent sneaks in, sees a weakness such as a lack of discipline, and then knocks him out. Every day is a battle, so you must prepare for war. Even when the enemy strikes, you are ready because you are well-equipped, well-trained mentally, and you are doing it consistently.

Second, start today with the scripture you have chosen to memorize by speaking it over your life and your family before you walk out the door. Say it again at lunch, again at dinner, and until it becomes so natural that you are carrying it through in every area of your life. Suit up, lace up, and get in the game. Playing is the only way you will know if you are even capable of winning. Decide today that you want to be a contender!

Life Application:

What you visualize for your life is important, but what you speak into your life is what bears fruit. You create your own barriers with your way of thinking. If you keep things in front of you that you want to come to pass and continually speak them, you will speak it into existence.

- Get index cards and write down the things you want to accomplish and speak them out loud DAILY. Write them in present tense. Example: "I am the CEO of my company." This active approach stirs up your faith. This is not I am wishing, but this is who I am... I see it, I breath it and I deserve this. I am capable! When you are reading over them, you are speaking life into them and belief in your heart. You are creating the life you want by seeing, speaking, and developing a belief that will in turn create a pattern of taking all the necessary steps of making your dream a reality.

Fitness Tip:

- Be accountable to yourself. Decide today why working out and developing good-eating habits is important to you. Write it down and this will be your fuel to get your engine started.

Day 2:

"Dust it off and Shine Bright Like a Diamond."

"Do you have eyes but fail to see, and ears but fail to hear? And don't you remember?"

-Mark 8:18 (NIV)

What is your vision this morning? What are you focusing on? Are you stuck on the don't (s) and can't (s) in your life? If so, this is an indication of where you are mentally. What your mind is focused on is what your life is living out. It is time to pull out the hardware and shine it up or the old pictures to remind you of the good times in your life. If you are a person that is saying I can't remember many good times, it is time to start creating some, don't you think?

At some point, you have to shake it off and say enough is enough; I deserve better and I want it now. It's through your challenges that change can occur, but only you can decide if that will be for the better or for the worse. Listen to your heart and be still to hear the whispers of God telling you it is time for you to move forward and follow the plan that is written across your heart. If you don't have that feeling or nudge that tells you that there is more to life for you and something that you are specifically designed to carry out, sit still, pray, and listen. Start putting up pictures to remind you of your strength, where you've been, and what you have accomplished. Do this so you can remember you are worthy and then rebuild the faith and hope of winning and living abundantly inside of you.

I remember when I was overweight and depressed; I'd just moved to Nashville. I went from being a 'mover and shaker' as a Hollywood mom to a stay at home mom. I looked up and I was overweight and very unhappy. One day, I went in my office and I sat there and cried. My husband put up all of my pictures from my Michigan basketball days, to Hollywood red carpets, articles, and family pictures. When I took the time to look around and really remember all the great memories, it gave me strength and hope again. I literally began to dust myself off. I took a stand that day that I was created to do great things, and that I have and I will continue. I began that day fasting and praying for God to show me the next phase of life.

"Weeping may endure for a night but Joy comes in the morning"

-Psalm 30:5 (NIV).

Dark times and doubt may come, but we have to be willing and open to the signs that it is time to rise and shine. Get up, get out of your funk, and make it happen. Rekindle the things found within that made you happy and feel alive. Take out old trophies, rewards, and accomplishments knowing that they are meant to be your starting point of your capabilities and your road map to victory. To produce the things you want on the outside, you must first be able to see those things you want on the inside. Create the visuals you need to see to carry you to the places you are supposed to be.

Life Application:

It is important to always have a "can do" and a "conquering" mentality to overcome the things that will come against us on a daily basis. The way to have this is to be reminded of your capabilities and the many things you have already overcome and achieved in your life.

- Get out the old chest with pictures of happy times and accomplishments in your past and put them in a collage where you can see them daily.
- Dust off the old awards, even if it was in the first grade, and shine them up. Remember how that moment felt when you received it and know that you can again capture that moment.

Fitness Tip:

Learn to spice up the water! Many times we don't drink it because it has no flavor, so we consider it boring. Instead of thinking of drinking water as a negative, consider the positives of water and what it is doing, to your body, as your body is consuming it. Water has no calories and is an appetite suppressant the helps the body metabolize stored fat. Drinking an adequate amount of water will help you with fluid retention, it helps to maintain proper muscle tone, keeps away constipation, and it aids in weight loss. So, consider water your friend and NOT the enemy. Add lemon, lime, mint, or your favorite fruit to help with the flavoring. I always think if it looks pretty, I am more susceptible to drinking it… it tricks your mind a little. Divide your weight in half and that is about the amount in ounces you should take in for your body on a daily basis.

Day 3:

"Being Healthy is a Choice and Not About Your DNA"

"Not by might nor by power, but by my spirit," says the Lord Almighty.

-Zechariah 4:6 (NIV)

Today, many of you speak to the sickness, depression, failed relationships, and addictions over your life. We give too much power to the almighty DNA. We are conditioned to think because high blood pressure runs in the family, that we too are more susceptible. Or if our parents got divorced, our chances are that much higher. When you think of being healthy, it is a combination of mind, body, and soul. You can look healthy on the outside and get a good report from the doctor, but still be sick with depression, and fear on the inside. We lock ourselves in a box instead of knowing we have the power to kick right through it.

"For God has not given us a spirit of fear, but of power and of love and of a sound mind".

-2 Timothy 1:7 (NIV)

We give up and give in before we give our selves the credit that we are created for much more. Your family does not set the path for your life. It is just one of many routes on the road map you can choose to take. If you looked at it as a dead end with no return, I bet you would decide to take another route. Choose the road you want to travel. It does not have to be one of over eating, depression, and lack of, especially in the world of so many alternatives today. So the blame is on you and not your mother or grandmother. Your family's decision does not have to be your curse; it can be your blessing of what not to do. Choose an area in your family history that you want to design another path for those who will follow you. Create a detour with a multitude of other great options.

Alter the outcome of what your kids and their kids will look at as their example. It is common to first look at your family history as a starting point for what is "in the bag." This curse may be in the family bag, but you do not have to pull it out of the bag for your life. Instead, add healthier choices and better decisions to "your" bag.

Instead of a litany of negatives, start a legacy of great things that you and your family can reset for generations to come. Because it has been done one way in the past, this does not mean it is the only way to be done in your future. What you will receive in your life is directly affected by your beliefs. You have to start today wanting and believing for bigger and better things. Raise your level of expectations knowing that God wants so much more for you, but first you must want it for yourself.

I am an only child whose dad never went to college and my mom, at 64, is back in school aspiring to get her college degree. It was never an option for my parents or for me to not go to college. They wanted me to start something different in our family that was not done by my grandparents or them. What I did see is hard work, determination, and lots of support in "my bag". I saw an opportunity to take what hasn't been done yet, and make it possible for the next generation. They too might have the courage to do it, because it has been done. Look for ways to redefine your family tree and for making more options available to pull from "the bag." Not only did I go to college, but I received a full scholarship in basketball being the first female in our family to play. I started a legacy and reset the standard for my own family. Decide today to not limit yourself by what has been done before you, but believe that you are the one to ADD life to the "family bag".

You can be the detour that helps redirect the lives of many.

Life Application:

It is important to not just exist and go through the motions as we talked about before. It is like driving in a car with no set place to go. Many of you are living your lives every day letting the day determine where you are going. Today you are going to map out the direction you want your life to go in. It is important to live life on purpose with a plan each and every day.

On construction paper, (be creative with your road map) mark your current place, and be strategic about where your current destination will be and what it looks like. What comes along with this? Ex: My destination is called Paradise Island. Here exists my vacationing, debt free life, seeing all my son's college games, spending girl time with my girls, and living life on my terms. I put all the things on my road map that, are currently in my life, and can get me there. Know that this road map is not your final stop. As in life, we get to the destination and God will give us our next direction to go in or adds layers to the destination. So don't just think you arrive and then that is it. Keep track, daily, of what your current stop is and where you are headed, so that you can be purposeful in your actions and decisions. Are your choices on course with where you are going or not? It is important to stay the course.

Fitness Tip:

Write down the exercises you like to do and the ones you don't like to do. Know how each exercise helps your body so that when you decide to do them, you know what body part you are working. For example: the exercise I dislike is running. I have run so much as an athlete in school, so I am over it. I do understand the benefits of running and that it changes my body the quickest. So the things we shy away from can help us the most. When you realize this, it helps you to be more apt to do them…knowing that they help affect you positively in the end. Find ways to incorporate them in a fun way so that it isn't a chore, but a choice. Study-chart those exercises you like on the left and the ones you don't like so much on the right. Work in a dislike once a week in place of your normal exercise of choice to switch it up and as a way of getting it in, but not having to over do it. As you begin to fit it in, you will see it really is not as bad as you think…especially when you see results.

Day 4:

"Meet Me at Baggage Claim"

"Do not conform to the pattern of this world, but be transformed by the renewing of your mind. Then you will be able to test and approve what God's will is—his good, pleasing and perfect will."

-Romans 12:2 (NIV)

I was lying in my bed trying to go to sleep when God gave me this; it was so clear that I had to get up and type it out in my phone notes. How often do you hear the phrase 'meet me at baggage claim?' Have you ever stopped and wondered how chaotic baggage claim really is? Not only is everyone vying for the front to take his or her bags off first, but there is the whole confusion of 'is that your bag or isn't it?' They all tend to look alike and hold all the individual mess that we have stuffed them with. Sometimes, you might have even thought it might be nice to pick up the wrong bag just to see what stuff someone else puts in theirs'. You will probably just see they travel with a lot of junk too!

God showed me how symbolic all of this is. When you are amongst others that look just like you, you are masking who you are and blending in. Have you heard the saying, "if you are the smartest in your group then you need to change groups?" It is because you might be teaching, but you are not being taught. You have to want to be stretched. It may feel uncomfortable, but in most cases, it is necessary. All of those bags on the belt at baggage claim tend to look alike which can cause a lot of questions to be raised just like when you are trying to blend in with a particular group. You lose your uniqueness and vibrancy. It is important to dare to be authentic and stick to what feels natural to you. Don't be so quick to conform.

When you know that something is yours and belongs to you, it is because there are distinct things that stand out and make it yours. At the sound of your child's voice or the touch of a loved one, you can instantly relate to who it is. This is the same when it comes to living out your life; you want it to be done your way so that your steps and way of going about it are a pattern like no other and it screams: 'this is ALL ME!' You don't want the same dream and blessings as everyone else. God can bless you the same, but it will show up differently. Everyone can get to the same destination, but the journey there has different routes.

When you go in your closet, your alone time to really dig in, unpack, and see what you are really dealing with is when you see what makes you who you are and sets you a part. It is in the separation when you can decipher who you are. Stop meeting at baggage claim and settling for blending in. You were created special in the image of God. Let go of the business of just doing and existing in effort to embrace your desired being. Be who you desire to be and it is never too late. Renew your mind and do not conform to what everyone else is doing. No more being mistaken, treated like the others, and being over looked. Be **Bold** and **STAND OUT**.

It always says a lot to me about someone that chooses to put a ribbon on their bag or a bold piece of tape. It says right away that they want to stand out and not be confused with the rest. They understand the importance of the littlest detail that will get their bag noticed. I am sure they carry this over into their lives in many ways by doing the little things differently.

Decide today that you will not be like everyone else. Dare to be different and to be original. Enjoy your individualism! It takes confidence and awareness to realize that doing the same thing will continue to give you the same results and emptiness that is better known as insanity! No more settling for: 'Is this my bag?' 'Is it my turn?' 'Why do I feel lost?' No more waiting in frustration. Start today by deciding to do the little things to separate yourself and make it easy to see exactly who you are.

Life Application:

The hardest thing about separating yourself from the rest is realizing the gifts you possess inside and what talents you have to set you apart that simply define you. It becomes a passion once you discover your purpose. What is it that makes you different? How can you exude this in a natural way that compliments the person that you are? Do you know what you are passionate about? It is important to raise your awareness about your strengths by understanding what they are and how you use them. Then you are able to apply them in every area of your life to make a difference.

We often forget the hard work we put in once what we have worked so hard to achieve has been accomplished and it is over. It is important to recall these strengths to help us see the power we have within and that we can do it again. Be a difference maker and start a movement that someone would be proud to follow.

- Do this exercise in your career, relationships, finances, health, and spiritual life.
- Name a time that you achieved a goal you set out to achieve in each of those areas of your life and you accomplished them.
- What did you do to make this happen? What strengths did you have to rely on to help carry it out?

Ex. Career- You received a promotion you wanted. You did this by studying someone in that position and asked for advice, worked later, you were creative in projects, and got up earlier to get into work, ahead of time, to get a jump-start. These are all the things that set you apart and helped you stand out so that you were picked for the job.

- Highlight what you did and the outcome. Most of the time it is being creative, diligent and decisive that you deserve it. Now decide today after this exercise that you will continue to live life everyday this way. Be up for the challenge and want to win. Winning is always being true to yourself and knowing you are living everyday being your best. Yes you are a winner!

Fitness Tip:

The most important thing in staying with the healthy choices you have made or your new workout regimen is to start out realistically. If you are not one to go to the gym on a daily basis, don't commit to five days a week. Set small goals to achieve so you can reward yourself with adding on a little more. You must have the feeling of achievement to want to keep doing what you are doing. Don't sabotage your progress by starting out too big. Small steps can add up and get you there faster instead of trying to take big ones that you are not ready for.

- Write down the time and day that fit into your schedule, consistently, every week.

- Instead of always thinking of the reward system, think of punishment to help you stay on track. If you miss a day, try to fit it in another day. If you do not get in what you set as your goal for the week, give yourself a" punishment" that you have to stick to and be honest with yourself. Ex. I missed my workout yesterday, so, today, I owe myself 20 pushups, 20 jumping jacks, and 20 squats. Your punishment still turns out as a way of rewarding yourself and making you feel good that you made it up. It can also set a standard that you don't like to be punished, so either way, you make it happen! You owe it to yourself to stay on track mentally and physically. Creating win-win situations is the best way to stay the course.

DAY 5:

"Be Ready To Receive"

"They will receive blessings from the Lord and vindication from God their Savior".

-Psalm 24:5 (NIV)

Wow! This scripture should have you running around the house this morning. If you would stand on the promise each and every day, you would take so much worry and stress out of your life by understanding that God has a blessing waiting for you and that whatever/whoever has wronged you, you will be vindicated! So the battles are not yours to fight… only to win! He has your back! He will make your wrongs right! Time is constantly being wasted on what you did not do or should have done; let that go! If He is a forgiving God, the only person holding you back to receive the blessing is you. Take your eyes off of what was and fix them on what is to come when you decide it is yours for the taking. God says you will receive a blessing and you ought to wake up everyday ready to receive!

It seems like just yesterday when I received one of the biggest blessings that God has ever given me: my daughter Cierra, also known as 'CeCe.' If I were not open, felt worthy, ready, and listened, I would have missed it. I was sitting in my car at the mall, which it was my first time ever going to that particular mall since it is not on my side of town. It was right before a fitness competition, and I simply needed to make a quick dash in and out to grab some running shoes to take on the trip for the next day. Well, as I got in the car and started it, I heard God say, "Get out the car."

Stay with me because this is a true blessing and I need you to get this, because I don't want you to miss the whispers of God. I get out and there is a Caucasian lady and her daughter pushing a stroller. We were the only people in the parking lot. This was like out of a movie; I could not have written this myself. When God sets it up, He leaves no stone unturned. All I could think to say was "Is that a baby doll you are pushing?" The baby was so tiny and they had her covered up, so she could not be seen.

Let me go back a little further. Prior to this, a girlfriend had called me and said she had a dream I had a little girl. At this time, I had CJ and with me being an only child, just having one child was fine with me! Then on a separate occasion, for those who believe in the gift of prophecy that is spoken in the bible as one of the many spiritual gifts (1 Corinthians 12:1-11), I received a prophecy that I was going to have a little girl. Remember, I am good with my one, so I thought everyone was a little off, but God is always true. The lady hesitated, but came over to me and said it was a little baby girl and she was her foster parent.

I looked at her, cried, and held her in my arms. I called the adoption agency from the parking lot and told them that I'd just seen my baby girl in a parking lot! They were a bit confused and thought I was crazy until I calmed down and explained that this baby is supposed to be my daughter. I was not at the mall for shoes! God was setting me up for much more than a simple purchase; He was connecting me with something that would be everlasting, my daughter. Cierra Danielle Sanders is what we named her three weeks later! God has it all ready for you, how it will be worked out, and at the specific time! But are you listening to His whispers? Are you ready to receive his ultimate blessings?

BE READY TO RECEIVE DAILY! You never know when or how God is going to bless you, but be expectant and this requires waiting on it everyday. Wake up thanking Him in advance for the blessing He will bestow upon you today and all you have to do is listen and take heed. Don't miss out on the good things that God has for you by thinking you are not worthy, or that you haven't been blessed in a while, so He must have overlooked you. No! He needs you ready and He wants you willing! Many blessings are missed because we get too busy, and don't trust His timing. They come in so many shapes and forms that even the littlest things such as waking up and being able to walk, talk, and read are blessings within themselves. Be thankful for the little things first, and the bigger things are sure to follow. Look daily for the blessings, and know that you are vindicated and worthy to receive all God has for you!

Life Application:

It is easy to get stuck in the daily grind and overlook the simple things and blessings of God. Every day, it is important to give thanks as a reminder of the goodness of God in preparation for what's to come. Before we can be ready, we have stop beating ourselves up over the past and know that God is a forward God. It is time that you join Him and move forward.

- Write down a blessing that was life changing for you. Take time to thank God again for His blessing and pray that you will be ready to receive, daily, all that He has for you.
- Write down something that you have not forgiven yourself for or have not stopped beating yourself up over.
- Now white it out and write 'Forgiven!' Done!

Fitness Tip:

It is important to keep a food log and fitness journal to stay on track with when and what you are eating along with the body parts you are training to not over train or over eat.
- Go get a small notebook and in the front of it, keep your food log.

-Track the time you ate, the meals, and try to eat three small meals and two or three snacks.
- In the back of the journal, keep track of what you are doing for your workouts such as: exercises, weights, reps, cardio, and how you felt before and after the workout

Tracking all of this information makes it easier to plan your meals and your workouts to see what you have already done and track what works for you. It helps knowing how you felt before and after the workout, so you can see you usually always feel accomplished and better after working out.

DAY 6:

"Do More to Be More"

"Whatever you do, do your work heartily, as to the Lord rather than for men, knowing that from the Lord you will receive the reward of the inheritance. It is the Lord Christ whom you serve."

-Colossians 3:23 (NIV)

Many people are content with being average and doing enough to get by. They work just enough to not get fired and they are never concerned with the integrity of knowing that each and every day they are giving their best. What you put in is what you get out of anything that you do. God did not create you to be mediocre. He is not a 'get by' God. He is a God of abundance, and when you are performing in excellence, He blesses in excellence. He created you with the right tools and the knowledge to excel. In everything that you do, you are a representation of Him. When you go beyond what the average person does, they see the God in you. They declare you different. It really doesn't take much…aside from doing more than the average person and these days, most people are performing below average.

I always tell my son, who is very gifted in so many areas of his life, that he is chosen for a purpose bigger than the gift itself, so he can't take that lightly. Every touchdown or record set is glorifying God for His masterpiece and great workmanship that He created. It is so much bigger that you. Thank Him daily for the talent, the will, the accomplishments, and for choosing you to represent Him and do it well.

When you take what you do off of you, there is such a bigger purpose of why your excellence is important. You want to make your father proud of His daughter. I know making my earthly father proud was something important to me growing up, but now I understand it is even bigger than him. Although that was a great start, you owe it to the God who created a good work in you. It should never be about the performance in anything that you do, but the honor for God. When you realize that He could have easily given it to someone else, this alone will help you want to give Him praise.

When people see the hard work and effort you put in, they should be attracted to the God they see in you…the light that attracts them to you. We should be disappointed in ourselves for giving less than our best and letting Him and ourselves down when we just go through the motions. When you do more, you become more. A person of excellence, who does it effortlessly, is revered. You are deemed worthy of the honors that you receive. Don't give a little and expect much. Don't complain; do it with joy, because you can, and it is in you! You have what it takes!

Often times, the person next to you can see the excellence in you better that you can see it in yourself, but if you choose to settle, they will normally let you! Choose to do YOUR best and be proud doing it. Set high standards and go out every day working hard and doing above what everyone else is doing to get higher results. You know the gifts and talents that have been crafted in you, so use them wisely. God is not a God of limitations, so no more limiting who you are and what you want out of life.

Decide today that you will rest your head every night knowing that you gave that day your best and put your best foot forward. Everyday gets easier when you know that, tomorrow, you have a great measure to work with from the day before. Live to out do yourself everyday. You will enjoy seeing the places that God will take you, because you decided that you would give more so that you can be more. Work hard and enjoy the journey. No, it is NEVER too late!

Life Application:

Think about an area of your life where you have settled for less. How can you be more valuable and get a better outcome by knowing what you know now about setting your standards higher and being a reflection of God? God sees you as worthy, so you have to see yourself the same and do the necessary steps to tap into your greatness. No more settling for average; strive to be your best.

- Write down the area(s) you have settled in and the steps you will take daily to become your best in that area(s).
- Tell someone you trust your new commitment and let them keep you accountable.

Fitness Tip:

Make no excuses for not getting to the gym. Using your own body weight or working out to an exercise tape is a great way to burn fat and tone. It helps you to stick to your work out plan and allows you to switch up doing the same exercises in the gym. Equip your house with the following and you can have a home gym.

1. A DETERMINED MINDSET-Be willing to put in the work to get the results you want. A healthy life style should be the main goal.
2. Free weights
3. Stability ball
4. Mat
5. Resistance bands
6. Jump rope

DAY 7:

"BE AN ENCOURAGER"

"But encourage one another daily, as long as it is called today, so that none of you may be hardened by sins deceitfulness."

-Hebrews 3:13 (NIV)

Today, let's look to help someone else. God has a way of using people to help bless someone other than just through him. He is always looking to see if you are willing to step up to the plate and be used. There have been times when I know that God has tugged on you and you felt you could have helped someone, but you chose to let it be their battle. We all have. It is easier to say I have my own problems and center our lives amongst ourselves. You are only missing out on the true blessing that you can have simply by being an encourager. God needs you to help build people up, speak words of faith, and help them to declare victory over their lives. His voice is coming through you and your actions. It doesn't cost anything or hurt you to compliment or help an employee in an area they are lacking in. Look to be a confidence booster.

I realize now that God created me to be a point guard, because my gift was helping to assist and encourage someone else. I believe when I was younger, I thought it was my game…clearly it was NOT! Whenever I saw a teammate struggling, I would take time to go over plays or make sure I recognized when they did something outstanding and told them "good job." That put me in the position of "Captain". You are worthy to lead! When you are a self-less person, lead by example, and show others you also want them to succeed, you gain their respect; they trust you. They will want you to lead them because they sense that you know where you are going and what it takes. If we can always look daily to lift someone else up, simultaneously, we are putting our own lives into "BELIEF TERRITORY". If you want them to believe and be encouraged, this ensures that you will always be on the right track too. There are enough people condemning and pointing out flaws. Be an encourager! Look to uplift, identify the good, and announce the greatness of others!

Life Application:

Before you can encourage someone, you have to understand how important it is and the real effects it can have on your life. Look back at your own life and see when someone's words or action helped uplift you and get you through. If you can't recall any, look at how it felt to not have someone there and start by making sure that making a difference in the lives of others can start with you. Changing one life at a time can make a huge impact in the world.

- Write in your journal the name(s) of the person that has encouraged you in momentous times in your life.
- Pray for them, and pray that God will allow you to pay it forward and that someone will write your name, pray, and thank you one day for being an encourager.

Fitness Tip:

It is important to recap the week. Look at how far you have come and how it has deposited into the goals you have set out to accomplish.
- Write down how you feel and what you have gained from taking a stand to be consistent and discover all that great things that God has given you.
- Encourage yourself to work even harder next week and to look to help someone else do the same. Go get 'em girl!

DAY 8:

"Be Confident; He Will Come"

"Do not throw away your confidence; it will be richly rewarded. You need to persevere so that when you have done the will of God, you will receive what He has promised."

-Hebrews 10:35-36 (NIV)

How many times have you thought you have given all you have, believed as long as you could for something, but it seemed as if it was never going to happen? So, you threw in the towel and gave up hope. God wants you to be a winner and not a whiner. He made you a champion and not a chump. So, be uplifted spiritually and continue to stand in faith even if it's for a lifetime! Just when you feel the most exhausted is when the door is about to open or the gold will be struck.

You may be saying to yourself: 'I put in the necessary work, I believed, and I had faith that it would happen.' Great! All of that is just a small PART of the process. You MUST BE CONFIDENT. God will reward a person that is sure of what they want, sure of His word, and continues to persevere.

My inspiration for this devotion came from my four-year-old daughter, Cori (CoCo), while contemplating writing on confidence. I was in MY own bathroom getting ready for the day. Sometimes I might lock it because I can't put on deodorant, spray, or put on lipstick without her wanting to do the same thing I am doing. There is an emphasis on 'MY,' because by being an only child, I can be just a little territorial at times! Well, this particular morning, I did not lock the door, but she was trying to get in and couldn't, so she assumed it was locked. First, she started with, "Mom didn't I tell you? Mom, are you serious?" You have to know my CoCo to understand how she is so animated and such a little entertainer. I decided to give her a lesson in belief. I said, "CoCo, it isn't locked; you can open it! You can do anything you put your mind to." Well, she still couldn't open it, but she wasn't giving up. I knew what would do the trick. If she knows her mommy needs help, she would dig in and get me out! "CoCo! Help! Mommy needs help!" CoCo says, "Mommy, I am not the Prince; I am a girl!" Well, I guess you can say a girl knows her place! She is confident that when you NEED help, the Prince will come rescue you! As funny as this was, what a great lesson it is; be Confident that your prince is coming. Know that God makes no mistakes and wants to help you in every situation and He will see you through. His will and plan is perfect for your life, so strive daily with confidence knowing you are a champion.

Life Application:

Have you ever been so confident in something that no matter what someone else says, you would not budge on what you believed? That is confidence. No matter why you had confidence in that particular situation, you had it and there was nothing anyone could do about it. This is how we need to be in every situation of what God has for us. It goes beyond belief; you have to be confident! Know the promises of God and your confidence will rise!

- Look through the bible and write down some of God's promises in your journal.
- Pray that you will have the confidence to carry these out in your life.
- Begin speaking the promises that you have written down over situations that you have doubt in.

Fitness Tip:

Preparation is the key to a successful work out regimen and eating plan.
- Prepare your meals ahead of time. Separate them in containers so that you can easily grab and go.
- Write down your menu for the week on Sunday, so you don't have to think about what to eat and get hungry. Planning ahead cuts down on cravings and skipping meals.

DAY 9:

"The Check System"

"Guard the good deposit that was entrusted in you - guard it with the help of the Holy Spirit who lives in you."
          -2 Timothy 1:14 (NIV)

I like to keep myself in line with what I call the check system. This can be applied in many areas of your life to keep you on track with the will of God. You can decipher a good deposit by using your check system. I think everyone can agree that making a deposit into your account feels good. Anything that is adding to your life or giving you positive results is a system you want to keep following. This is why God says, *"Guard the good deposits with the help of the Holy Spirit"* (II Timothy 1:14, NIV). If you are growing, keep sowing.

You have to be careful of what you let stick with you. Whether it is a situation, people, or words, you are in control of what you keep and what you destroy. Literally: destroy it and let it go. You can make a deposit or you can dispose it. Don't let unworthy things take up space and not have enough room for the worthy ones. The deposits are the things that enhance your purpose and line up with your goals. This is your check system to continually uplift your spirit and keep you in line with what God says and not what someone else thinks. To be rich in what you are created to be, you have to guard your deposits. Always look to be a victor and not the victim. I say, "Bring me good or don't bring anything!"

Many of us have heard the cliché', "Check yourself before you leave out the door." I remind my kids every morning to check their eyes, breath, and their noses before leaving out of the house. This may sound funny, but it is the difference between wondering and knowing if you are presenting yourself to the best of your ability. My son says he goes to the restroom in between classes now to make sure he is together! I hope he isn't over doing it! I can recall times when I would get back in the car, looked in the mirror, and see if there was something on my face. If I would have looked before getting out, I wouldn't be so mad thinking about how I just had a conversation with someone with food or other particles on my face! Another thing that would drive my husband and kids crazy is when we would leave the house and I would ask if everything was turned off. Now, I make sure I check before I leave so I don't have to worry or wonder… I know it's done! I am sure you have done this about the curling iron, iron, or stove. No more second-guessing: use that check system!

The other area is to make a daily task. Checking things off of a list keeps you accountable to your word of saying you want to complete something. It is your own standard of daily accountability. It also helps to keep things in order in your mind and cut down on going through the motions. Being specific helps with the overall result of what you want to achieve.

For example: I have on my refrigerator daily task and chores for my kids. They are supposed to check off what they do everyday. Now, do they always do it? No, but I am at least creating a check system for them to adhere to. There are consequences for NOT following the system mommy has taken time to create. My main goal is teaching them to first be responsible, to be accountable to themselves, and to develop good habits. What they also receive is a sense of accomplishment. The end result is always about the feeling you possess upon completing the task. It feels good to succeed and be a finisher. Start today by using the check system and guarding your deposits by creating good habits and letting bad habits go.

Life Application:

Creating check systems is the best way to balance what you need to accomplish in your life and keeping you accountable.

- Write in your journal some things you need to stop procrastinating about and start today to get done. If it is not important or necessary, take it off the list.
- Go back after checking them off and write how you felt once it was done. Remember that feeling and do it all over again in other areas of your life; recapture it again and again. Let that feeling of accomplishment chase you down.

Fitness Tip:

The best way to eat consistently is learning about the power of foods. It is important to eat for fuel and not simply for pleasure. Think about the foods that you are putting in your body on a daily basis and ask yourself, "Is this charging me up or weighing me down?"

- Make sure you are incorporating the right foods and amounts to properly fuel your body.
- Go to www.choosemyplate.gov for excellent choices, to learn food groups, and understand why it is important to have the right amount of each food group for your

body. This is an excellent resource for understanding the importance of what you eat and the importance of adopting exercise as a lifestyle.

DAY 10:

"Push Through with Passion"

"Do you see a man who excels in his work? He will stand before kings; he will not stand before unknown men."

-Proverbs 22:29 (NIV)

Have you ever been truly passionate about something that you were doing? Didn't you realize it came easier and didn't feel like it was weighing you down even if it was tough or challenging to you? When you follow the voice within and follow your heart when it comes to making choices in life, you are lining up with what you believe, what it is you truly want, and usually your life's purpose. The hardest task is believing, "Is this for me? "Am I ready? Am I equipped? When you see it and can almost taste it, especially over and over, then it is for you. 'If you can see it, you can be it'…we have all heard that before. Believe it is the prescription God wrote out for you to experience through your eyes only!

The perfect time to jump right in and get started is when you first see it and feel it. Even if you don't have all the resources available at the moment, write down the vision and God will supply the rest. He has already made provisions for you on how it will all come to pass. God has designed you precisely to run the race that you are supposed to run. You were not made to live 'average.' If it seems like a grand idea, you are on the right track. Your dreams are right where they are supposed to be when they scare you a little. So I say, go big or go home! This is what He has worked out for you, so excel before God. Your limits are not defined within man; they are within you. You are meant to do big things, so don't short change yourself and making yourself seem small.

People who follow their passions are excited about what they are doing. They feel a sense of purpose and enjoy doing it. It becomes about helping and benefitting others and not just yourself when you are passionate about something and it serves a purpose. Your purpose, which is a result of your gifts, provides a motive for and is valuable to the advancement of others. When you see that it is valuable and you can put a price on it, this is called good business.

I was in New York having dinner with Luther Vandross and a friend of mine, and yes, I could barely eat because I was so excited about dining with 'thee' Luther Vandross. Someone came to our table and asked him to sing a little bit of a song for them. His response was, "my voice is my gift and I can't take that lightly. I get paid to sing." At first I didn't understand it, but now I do. If he went around singing for free all of the time, his value would go down. Protect your value; your gift is to be valued. Don't be afraid to put a price on it. Some things are for free and some things come with a fee!

I remember when God gave me the vision for a restaurant. I could hardly sleep. I had never been in the restaurant business, so I had no idea really where to get started. Understand that when you follow your heart, attacks will come. Talk about heart attacks! I heard this from a pastor and it is so true now when I look back on that time. When you are following your ambition, the devil will come to attack you because he sees where you are going and wants to cut you off before you get there. Most people quit when the attacks come, because they don't want to deal with the pressure or the thoughts of failure. Failure is when you give up. Falling a few times might happen, but learn how to fall forward, look up, and get up. The biggest lessons are in our failures not our success! You are not a failure…EVER. Learn from mistakes and don't let them over take your vision and cause you to give in.

I had to surround myself with people who were good in the areas that I was not good in to help my vision come alive. Don't be afraid to ask for help or be mentored by someone that has been successful in what you want to do. In my push to complete it, I had to be passionate and not go through the motions. You want to give your all so that you can feel good about the hard work you put in to achieve it. Let your passion shape your purpose and help bring the plan into fruition.

Through all the firings, codes, and wrong orders, I kept going because I was passionate about what this restaurant would do for families. It became bigger than owning a restaurant. As I've stated before: the best feeling you can have is when you understand your gift is serving someone else. That kept me going. Let what you do become bigger than you and getting your feelings hurt or your hands dirty. Keep your eyes focused on the end result. If you keep seeing it, your vision will become a reality.

So wherever you are and whatever you want to do, be passionate. Let that burning desire within drive you to keep going to pursue your goals with excellence. The next time you have to push through, and you really want it, let your passion take over the wheel. Remember your purpose and why you have the desire and know that the passion will take you there.

Life Application:

There is nothing like the feeling of giving your best to something and it is serving a purpose as you are living with a purpose. It is important to take time out to see how you are carrying out your plan in life. Are you living every day on purpose? What areas are you passionate in and what areas do you need to give more passion to if you are going to finally reach your end result?

- Write down the answers to these questions in your journal.
- Write down something you have been seeing and wanting to do but haven't had enough faith and courage to try. Find a scripture about fear and courage such as Deuteronomy 31:6. Memorize it and pray it over the desires of your heart so that you will step out and bring them into existence.

Fitness Tip:

The best way to not get bored is to keep what you are doing fresh and learn new things to add to it.

- Learn a new healthy recipe that you can cook and incorporate it into your new healthy choices. Take a class to teach you new ways to cook healthy for you and your family.
- Start making a healthy recipe book so that the recipes you like are accessible at all times; share them with a friend.

DAY 11:

"Become Unstuck"

"The Lord has done it this very day; let us rejoice today and be glad.

-Psalm 118:24 (NIV)

How easy is it to get stuck in a routine? It can be a choice we make because we have been conditioned by our family history, or we have just become so 'regimented' that we forget to slow things down a little in an effort to enjoy learning and exploring new avenues. God says, for us to rejoice and be glad in each day! It is hard to do this when life becomes stale, and we get stuck in a rut. We begin to make our days have no meaning with no anticipation and nothing new to look forward to; we begin going through the motions. You know the feeling: existing and with no excitement. We even catch ourselves saying, "Same thing …different day"!

Today is the day to make it less mundane. Start by taking a different way to work to start your day off with change. Choose another option on the lunch menu today or make something different than the spaghetti you make every Thursday. When you choose new options, you begin to refresh and bring about newness in your life. Your life can start taking on that new car smell, and you can feel renewed and more alive. You should wake up every day having something to anticipate or arrive to. Get out of bed wanting and desiring to enjoy the day and making each one count. You will begin to discover that you are versatile and that you are adaptable.

We, as women, tend to complain about the patterned life we live, yet we are afraid of spontaneity. Go to bed tonight with a little something sexier on for your spouse or cook dinner in heels and a cute outfit! Take out the mommy part of your day if you are a mom, and enjoy your womanhood first. It feels good to feel like a queen and a lady. When you adhere to that first, you will treat yourself that way. Remember: whatever you indulge in the most, is how you define yourself. Decide to be the sexiest and fulfilled you, FIRST, before being a mom or anything else.

There will be several things that will come at you to throw you off course. The two main ingredients to equip yourself with are: adaptability and resilience. You won't give in or freak out when something didn't go exactly as planned, because you have learned it is important to be adjustable and you believe in bouncing back. Your outcome is always determined by your response. You have conditioned yourself to be flexible when you need to. You won't be afraid of the detour sign, because you realize that you can still get to your desired destination. Practice and sharpen these muscles now so that you can become 'unstuck' and begin to become unstoppable. Look to tune in, first, to your strength channel and not your stress channel.

Coming from a football household, this is better known as an audible. When the quarterback lines up to the line of scrimmage and he notices the defense is doing something different than what he expected, he yells out a new play. Sometimes we need to change the plays in our own lives and call an audible at the last minute to make a life-changing decision. Don't be afraid of change, as this will allow you to be stretched and challenged to new heights. If you keep seeing the same outcome, if you feel you are not growing, and you are not feeling excited about life, it is time to become unstuck and switch it up! Your way is not the only way! See what is working for someone you admire, and add a little of that spice to your life. Just because you are accustomed to doing something one way, does not mean it is the only way you can get it done!

Don't allow life to become so monotonous that you don't take time to enjoy it. Take the scenic route to work today, or go to the mall or a new boutique and browse leisurely to discover something new about your choice of style. Don't be so rushed today to pick the same color that you have decided looks good on you and your closet is already full of. Try a new hair color or style! Bring something new to you TODAY; stop thinking about it and be about it. Look to fulfill new meaning in your life daily. Give yourself a reason to want to take on the day and be ready for it with some spontaneous savvy. Challenging yourself to make these small changes will help you begin to look forward to experiencing every day as a new day and not just as another day. Renew the pep in your step and let them see a new swagger about you!

Life Application:

It is easy to forget to smell the roses and savor the good things. We are so busy rushing to get from one thing to the next that we miss out on so many opportunities we can enjoy and be thankful for along the way.

- Take time to think about how your life has become monotonous in certain areas. Write down what you are going to do differently to switch it up and enjoy it more.
- Take the scenic route today and leave early so that you are not rushed. Take time to smile and breathe easy.

Fitness Tip:

Oh how easy is it to plateau in your weight and to get bored with your workout routine! Doesn't it seem as if it happens fast? Look to add something different to your workout today and get past the boredom and break through the plateau.

- Park further away so that you have to walk farther.
- Take the steps instead of the elevator.
- Do interval training instead of a steady pace. Walk/run-walk/ run, or jog/sprint-jog/sprint. Do these for short bursts of 30 seconds, or one to two minutes and see if you will feel different and get different results.
- Do a different workout routine from a magazine or from a suggestion a friend gave to you.

DAY 12:

"What's Your Reason? What Do You Want?"

"In the beginning, God created the heavens and the earth."

-Genesis 1:1 (NIV)

I'm sure you are thinking, "What does the title have to do with the scripture?" If so, the answer is: Everything. In the beginning, when God was completing His task, He knew what and why He was doing what He was doing. Everything God does is strategically planned and has a perfect ending. He didn't have it thought out one day and threw something together the next day in the hopes that it would work out. He knew His mission and everything He did fit into the completion of it.

What is your reason for getting up everyday? Why do you do what you do? If you don't have a reason for waking up every morning and giving your best to each day, this may explain your depression, mood swings, or lack of zest. Not only is it important to have a reason, you have to know what you want and then it is easier to know why you want it. Is it a better life for your kids, living a debt free life, or being your own boss one day? There has to be something that drives you and keeps you going when the days come that you don't feel like going on. There are days when you second-guess yourself and ask, "Why do I do, what I do?"

It all comes back to the desire and the fire that should be burning inside of you and that leads to the purpose defined by your existence. Ask yourself now, "am I doing what I feel I am called to do?" If not, "why not?" Repeating the same thing day after day and not fulfilling the desires of your heart is like a leaking faucet. It will drive you crazy until you decide to fix it. It is time to start living in the 'what I want' instead of living in the 'what I have to.' If coaching, teaching, speaking, singing in the choir, or volunteering is something you like to do, you need to find a way to fit them into your life. Find a way to incorporate things that bring you joy, happiness, and put a smile on your face.

As a mother and a wife, what we enjoy takes the back seat and we even forget what that is anymore! We usually put our reason behind what we do or want for the family or the kids. I dare you to step out and take on something that makes what you are doing for YOU and ABOUT YOU! Trust me; it's ok! Maybe it is something you have wanted to do since you were a kid. Let it lighten you and bring a peace and laughter to your heart. When is the last time you laughed so hard you were in tears? Let loose and laugh it off! The next time you feel like crying try laughing and see how laughter alters how you feel.

Don't feel guilty in enjoying some of the things that bring you pleasure and define you more than your title at work or being a mother, wife, daughter, and friend. God gave you a purpose *Greater* than that. Look at all the pieces that make up your amazing life's puzzle that you live. Enjoy being all of you, for all of your reasons, and take in all of the desires of your heart. I can still hear my dad telling me, "Do what you have to until you can do what you want to do." I believe you can get fulfillment by doing them at the same time. Let the "have to" drive you into achieving the "want to".

Life Application:

Today, have an attitude of gratitude! Be thankful for another day that God chose to include you in; you are a part of His reason. Decide what you want out of the day, out of life, and out of the things you are doing daily. The next time you are faced with a difficult day at work or in your personal life, remember why you are doing what you do and what you are working to get to! If you don't know your reason for waking up every morning and what you want out of life, it is time to think about it, discover it, and write it down.

- What are you doing daily that you enjoy doing?

- What is something you have always wanted to do but aren't doing? What steps can you take to make it possible?
- Think about the things you have to do right now for whatever reason. How much longer will you settle for doing it? Do you have an exit strategy?

Fitness Tip:

The easiest way to stay on a fitness regimen is incorporating the things you enjoy doing.

- Do something today that you enjoy doing and see it as beneficial for your fitness regimen.
- Do something that is nostalgic…something you haven't done in a long time but maybe enjoyed as a kid. I.e.: Double Dutch, skating, dancing, hopscotch, tug-of-war, or dodge ball.

DAY 13:

"KEEP THE LIGHT ON"

"You are the light of the world. A town built on a hill cannot be hidden. Neither do people light a lamp and put it under a bowl. Instead they put it on its stand, and it gives light to everyone in the house. In the same way let your light shine before others, that they may see your good deeds and glorify your father in heaven."

-Matthew 5:14-16 (NIV)

In the world we live in today, with cancer on the rise, the economy being down, and our children being led by social media and ads, it is hard to see the light at the end of the tunnel. I remind myself daily that no matter what anyone else is doing, I have to let my light shine. I cannot give in to the temptations of the world and what everyone else is doing. God needs someone to take a stand and not be ashamed to be different.

The scripture for this devotion is what I have on my kid's vision board. I think it is important for everyone to be reminded of a scripture that will get them through the current phase of their lives. My oldest two are teenagers and this is not an easy stage to be in right now considering peer pressure and hormones that are on the rise. I talk to them about the challenges of being called a leader. God has truly called some people to be leaders whether they want it or not; it is their gift. What they choose to do with it is up to them. There are some people that possess contagious spirits and ways that make others gravitate toward them; this is my son. I tell him that no matter what everyone else is doing, you have to always keep your light on. People are always watching and if you turn it off, that is when they are paying the most attention.

People really do want someone to take the leadership role, have a sense of control, and help guide them in the right direction. It is hard for most people to stay consistent and stay connected on their own. We all need someone who will keep us motivated and become our example of hope. My kids, like most kids, go through the typical teenage emotional roller coaster, but their choice is not to cuss, drink, smoke, and have sex because they want to represent God well. They realize that making good choices can help to positively influence others.

In the middle of it all, when it seems like you are going through a tough season, remember all of the good seeds you have planted and stay diligent because your season will come. Your harvest will rise, so keep the sun shining. God is seeing if you are keeping your light on even when it is dark…or are you choosing to blend into the darkness? It is not the time to hide; it is time to seek and to find! He has put a light in each of us to, as scripture notes, 'shine amongst the hilltops.'

Wherever you go, never feel like you have to lessen yourself so that you can make someone else feel comfortable or feel better. You are just masking who you really are and if that is you, I want you to feel so uncomfortable that you want to scream and just burst out to be who you really are! Take pride in your life choices of who you represent and want to be. Always be the authentic you and learn to love the skin that you are in.

One of my favorite poems is by Marianne Williamson and it is entitled, "Our Deepest Fears". I have this on my mirror and each of my children has it on theirs. It speaks so well about how our fear is usually the fear of success and truly being ourselves in our own uniqueness. Don't fear to live in greatness. You were designed to be great! When you give yourself permission to be your best, you unconsciously are telling others to do the same. God gave you an individual light to shine, and He wants you to embrace your gifts, talents, and the beauty you have inside and share it with the world.

Life Application:

Wow! Doesn't it feel good to know that you are a light... a star to shine brightly in this world? What are you going to do with the light that is within you?

- Answer the question above in your journal.

- Copy and print out the poem below, put it on your mirror and read it daily to remind yourself of the calling that God has on your life.

Our deepest fear is not that we are inadequate.
Our deepest fear is that we are powerful beyond measure.
It is our light, not our darkness
That most frightens us.

We ask ourselves,
Who am I to be brilliant, gorgeous, talented, fabulous?
Actually, who are you *not* to be?
You are a child of God.

Your playing small
Does not serve the world.
There is nothing enlightened about shrinking
So that other people won't feel insecure around you.

We are all meant to shine,
As children do.
We were born to make manifest
The glory of God that is within us.
It's not just in some of us;
It's in everyone.

And as we let our own light shine,

We unconsciously give other people permission to do the same.
As we are liberated from our own fear,
Our presence automatically liberates others.

- Marianne Williamson

Fitness Tip:

There are times that we don't seem to have enough time in the day to get in the meals that we need… let alone making the right choices when we are on the go. Staying on your eating regimen requires that you make the right choices 95 % of the time.

- I have always taken a protein shake or meal replacement shake to get my meals in and to make sure I am feeding my body as many well-balanced meals as possible. Incorporating a good meal replacement shake or bar will do that.
- There are so many out there, so read the labels and ask your friends what their favorites are and what has been working for them. I use Advocare's products which has been around for 20 years. They have their own Sci-Med board, so I know the quality is top notch and it tastes good. To see some of the choices they offer, you can refer to my website at www.advocare.com/11098958. This is what I use, but again, ask around and make your decision based on your likes and dislikes. Including this in your daily eating plan is important.

DAY 14:

"KNOW YOUR ROLE"

"Now to him who is able to do immeasurably more than all we ask or imagine, according to his power that is at work within us."

-Ephesians 3:20 (NIV)

When CJ was about ten years old, I helped coach his youth summer basketball league. We were the only team that included a girl as one of the players and most of them had never played before. So, in essence, we started with minimal options from the very beginning! Expectations for our team were pretty much non-existent as other teams were loaded and ours was 'thrown together.' At first, the kids were not happy that their coach was a mom and let alone a GIRL. When they found out I played college ball and that I could beat any of them in one-on-one, I gained a little more respect.

The first game was a disaster with turnovers, traveling, and no one felt comfortable enough to shoot the ball which is important in scoring. We only had two kids that would even shoot…one was CJ and the other was a kid who loved to shoot, but he couldn't get it near the rim. Yep! It was quite a disaster that needed desperate measures! This is when I decided it was time to give each of them a role to play on the team. Each of them had a nickname and now they knew where they belonged. There was no more guessing or trying to figure out what to do or where to be on the court. We went from being the "scrubs" to being champions with a girl on the team and a girl as the coach!

This is certainly relative to your life. You may be at work and feeling inadequate because you are the only woman on a power-filled team of men! You are in fact worthy and do not be afraid to show them you are strong and that you are proud of your womanhood! Yes! You do belong because that is where God has placed you! You might be feeling overlooked, under-appreciated, or like your worth is being down played, but what matters is that understand your role, and you understand your value!

In your family, do you feel like you are the "middle child" or the one that feels like you don't know where you fit in like the others? Have you found your role? My middle daughter, CeCe, struggles with this. I had to remind her that the same breath that breathed life and a purpose in her brother and sister did the same with her! Choose not to snooze and go through life complaining! The only thing you need to claim being in the middle of is your blessings! You matter, and what you have to offer matters. God gave you something to bring to the table that no one else can deliver like you. Once you find what that is and how to use it, you will understand the power that you have. You will have a sense of strength and will become empowered.

Remember the little boy on the team I told you who liked to shoot but couldn't hit the rim? He became my best rebounder and loved it! We have to find other ways to score! I explained to him that with his strength and his tenacious personality, he could be the "King of the boards". He loved the sound of that! He had a name, he had a purpose, and he conquered it! His mom wrote me a letter midway through the season and said how his grades had improved and for the first time, he wanted to go to practice and made sure she would not have him late. He was excited because he felt he was a part of something and he was making a contribution! He gained empowerment, and he understood his role. God can do immeasurably what you think cannot be done. He can use other people to help you discover the immeasurable gifts within. If you at least choose to do what you can first, He will fill in where you can't!

Think about your kids if you have them. What are you speaking over their lives? Do they know what they contribute to the family? Have you made their role clear and given them a sense of value? When you give positive reinforcement and allow someone to see their gifts and they see the rewards in using them, you are opening the flood gates to so much more. They gain a new sense of pride, willingness, and belief that will build other areas in their lives.

If you don't know your significance at work, in your family, or in your home, take time to ask your co-workers, or those that love you and know what they see in you. You might think you are good in one area, but you are actually great in another where you can be even more beneficial. Don't get caught up in what you think you should do over what you are best at doing. Find your place, discover your role, and do it well…be an asset.

Life Application:

It is crucial to who we are and what we can become to know what role we play on a team. Your work environment, family, and home life are your team. When you know where you stand and where you are valued the most, you realize what you do matters and you most likely, want to do it well to not be a disappointment. To function at your best is when you know that what you do counts and plays an intricate part in helping the team win.

- Write down the role you play in the different areas of your life.
- If you are not sure, ask someone you trust to find out what they see in you and what you can contribute to the best.
- Decide today that you will consciously bring your best to the table and make your role a

significant part of helping the team (i.e.: family, work, etc.) function to its highest capabilities.

Fitness Tip:

It is important to read food labels, but what is even more important is to understand what you are reading and how it can help or sabotage your eating regimen. Learning the simple things about reading food labels can be the difference in having a successful eating lifestyle and not.

- Go to a website and train yourself on reading food labels and then look in your pantry for the things you need to get rid of. Here is an example of one, but there are plenty to choose from. http://www.fda.gov/food/resourcesforyou/consumers/nflpm/ucm274593.htm
- Decide today to make better choices about what you have learned.

DAY 15:

"BE OBEDIENT"

"Do not merely listen to the word, and so deceive yourselves. Do what it says."

-James 1:22 (NIV)

How often, as a parent, do we say this to our children: "be obedient," or "do as I say; not as I do?" You want your children to not just hear you but to be a doer because you have their best interest at heart. So it is important for you to be a doer of what you preach! This is so true of how God feels about you. He always has your best interest at heart.

When was the last time you knew that God was telling you to do something, but instead, you put it off or didn't trust the voice inside to just do it? You should have called someone, gone to help someone with their move, given someone that sweater they said they loved so much and you barely wore anyway, or went to church and missed out on a word that you knew God had for you. These are a few examples of how simple the task could be, but we brush them off with "I know I should," but instead, you don't.

God wants you to pass the smallest tests. He

wants to trust you with the little things such as obedience in an effort to release the bigger things like the knowledge and the resources you need to fulfill a dream. If there is something you have been waiting to come to pass and it seems like you are almost there, obey the little things. If you feel like you haven't gotten blessed in a while, take your thoughts off of you and think about the little things you know God has been asking of you. Reach out to a loved one you haven't talked to in a while because of a disagreement. Be the bigger person to help become a better person. Be obedient to God not to your pride.

I can recall a few times that I heard God tugging at my spirit to do something that made no sense to me at the time, but it overtook me and became so heavy on my heart that I had to do it. The first time I had ever experienced the power of obedience was years ago while in church and God told me to give a lady a check. I did not know this woman and neither did she know me. I was almost a little embarrassed because I didn't know her situation. As much as I tried to ignore what I felt God was asking of me, I couldn't stay still in service. So, afterwards, I approached her. I apologized if I was offending her, but I told her that God told me to give her a check and I asked if she would accept it. When she opened it, she cried and told me it was the exact amount she needed by tomorrow or she would have been evicted.

Didn't that touch you? I was blown away!

My act of obedience truly blessed someone that day, along with myself. God used me to touch someone that needed to believe His power was real. We both saw the power of God work in our lives through being a doer that day. Listening and obeying is so important. Think of the times you might have missed out on blessing someone and experiencing the power of God by not being obedient to the tugging in your spirit.

    You need to make a choice today to never do that again. Don't miss what God has for you or being able to be used to help deliver someone else's blessing. Be obedient today and listen to the whispers of God telling you to be a doer of His word. Don't let business, fear, or doubt hold you back from connecting to the blessings and the dreams that God is ready to unlock for you! You have the key to be a world changer, so listen and obey.

Life Application:

It is so easy to hear but put off what you know God has asked of you. You let second-guessing create the "should you" or "shouldn't you (s)" or the waiting, keep you from being a blessing and in return getting blessed. It is important to start today by deciding to be a doer of what God is asking of you so that you can be the blessing that He needs you to be. He needs you as His connector. No more delaying your blessings and the blessings of others. Hook it up!

- Write, in your journal, the times that you know God has asked something of you and you have been putting it off.
- Act today on any of those things that you know you can still do and be a difference maker.
- Write down some blessings you have been waiting for and underneath that write: "I AM OBEDIENT AND A DOER OF GOD'S WORD. USE ME."
- When those things come to pass, check them off as part of your check system, and remember God's goodness whenever you have doubt to get you back on track.

Fitness Tip:

The best way to stay on track with a commitment is to have an accountability partner that can help motivate you and keep you on track.

Make sure it is someone that has goals themselves and wants you to also succeed with yours.

- Go to a group workout together. Enjoy working out and pushing each other to the next level.
- Make a healthy meal at home and sit down and enjoy it over girl time.

DAY 16:

"STICK AND STAY"

"Do not throw away your confidence; it will be richly rewarded. You need to persevere so that when you have done the will of God, you will receive what he has promised."

-Hebrews10:35-36 (NIV)

It is easy to say we are going to stick to something and stay the course when we are initially excited about it and confident. Then something comes and gives you a gut punch, so you start questioning your ability. God says, be confident! Remember what you saw as the end result even when the eyes you are looking through get blurry and the road gets foggy! Recapture the picture in your mind and make it clear again! You have to believe what you know and let it be that. It is the dream and promise given to you, so even the person closest to you may not see the sense in it, but it wasn't given to them in the first place. We expect someone to help us believe, but they can't even see it. It is not their glasses to look through or journey to travel; it is yours! God didn't give them the vision, the promise, or the tools to complete it; He chose it for you.

When you persevere and do your part, even when you have to go left but you want to go right, you have to know that God sees your effort and is clearing a path for you ahead. Don't stop before you get there; let Him work supernaturally on your behalf. He knows your heart and sees your hard work, so don't give in to a weak mind when God gave you a strong mind.

When my son was a part of the filming for the movie "Ray," I was amazed by what he did on set. I saw it with my own eyes. Jamie Foxx and the director, Taylor Hackford, told me that we should consider moving to LA because the movie was going to be huge for everyone in it. It was a big move for us because we were currently living in Nashville, TN. I decided to go simply "test the waters" and to see if what I believed could really happen. It seems like yesterday when we walked into the first agent's office and CJ was just six years old. They gave us a script with just a little time for him to go over and then he was to audition with the agent. I was nervous, he was nervous, and this was our first time ever having to rehearse and get him ready in such a short period of time. Well, he bombed it! We got the call from our Nashville agent that the LA agent informed them that he was "Green" and that we should go back to Nashville! Talk about harsh! Well, I cried and almost headed back.

Suddenly, the fight, determination, and strength that came out of me, is what took over the doubt and the fear. I remembered what I saw on set and I remembered what an Oscar winner and an

Oscar nominated director told me. That agent saw what she wanted to see that day; she didn't see what was to be! God showed me that! I could have let her block our blessings, but I decided to stick and stay. I saw and believed the path ahead would open and guide me where I knew God was taking us. I was on the wrong street with that agent and I'm glad I didn't decide to take her directions to get me where I knew I was going!

Do you follow me? You know where you need to go; do what you have to do to get there! The movie was huge and CJ was nominated for a NAACP award for best supporting actor against Jamie Foxx, Don Cheadle, and Morgan Freeman! He went on to do commercials, another movie, and a few hit series. If I would have left, I would have so many memories in a box that I wouldn't have had the opportunity to open. Claim your prize! The next time the going gets tough for you, don't fret! Pick your head up, trot harder, go harder, and you tell yourself, "I am here to Stick and Stay even if it takes me a lifetime, because I believe!"

Life Application:

I want to jump up and down all over again. There is nothing like believing and staying the course and reaping the rewards because you stuck with it! Was it tough? YES, but you did not let negativity and doubt take over you! That is what being a winner is made of! You dig deep, you put in the work, and you stay on course. Follow your heart…not even your head sometimes because it isn't always on straight. When you give your best, God will work out the rest.

- Write down in your journal something you let go and you still feel is for you. You might have let time, someone, or other things deter you away, but you can still see it clearly.
- Tell yourself that this time, you are going to stick and stay no matter what, because this is what you want and what God has shown you. Every day is a day closer to discovering your destiny. Every day and every choice you make takes you closer to or further from your dreams.

Fitness Tip:

The key to getting a workout in is not beating your self up about not having enough time. There is no set amount of time for a workout; it all matters and counts towards effort. Just be consistent in your effort and the rest will follow.

- You had a super busy day and you are tired, but you don't want to feel guilty about not working out. Do the following:
  - 20 minutes
  - Use your body weight and do back-to-back intervals to build up a sweat.
  - Jumping jacks, squats, lunges, push-ups, and dips. Repeat 3 x 15.
- You just burned calories and did great strengthening exercises and best of all, you end the day not feeling guilty that you missed a workout! A little can go a long way!

DAY 17:

"WHAT CHANNEL ARE YOU ON?"

"The mind of a sinful man is death, but the mind controlled by the Spirit is life and peace."
-Romans 8:6 (NIV)

A huge part of where you are right now in your life is what channel and level you are on mentally. You can't have negative thoughts and expect a positive outcome. You can't dwell on failure and expect success. Your thoughts control the outcome of your entire life. You have the ability to change what you see and depict the outcome. How many times have you created something in your mind, in advance, and even gave it a negative outcome? It hasn't even happened yet! We have all done it before…be honest! Well, you can do the same thing by seeing something in advance and giving it a winning and positive ending instead. Try practicing by choosing the scenes you have created, over and over in your head, and giving those scenes happy endings.

Ladies: most of us need to do this in our relationships! I know I am SO guilty of this in my own. I conjure up in my mind what I think my husband has done to the point that I give it life. He comes home and I have developed an attitude based on my thoughts! No matter what he says to change them, I have already played out what I believed happened because I control the remote in my mind! This has been the culprit to many failed relationships! It is the power of assumption! Try assuming great situations and him buying you the perfect gift or surprising you with dinner! Don't go over his talents, but you can determine the outcome of your relationships by controlling your emotions and how you see it! Give your relationships permission to succeed and deem yourself worthy of having a healthy one! Whew! That was for me! No matter what examples you have or don't have the example of a long-lasting and loving marriage can start with you!

You have the power to control the peace and harmony of your life. You can control who comes in and who goes out. You can control what you want and what you don't want. What you see is what you will believe you are capable of. If you can't see it, then for sure, you can't be it. So, give yourself the strength and the power to be a champion. Have your channel set on super woman ruling the world and creating world peace. If you start there you will go out with a new attitude and conquering spirit.

Decide today that every morning you are going to set your mind on the right channel. Choose success, happiness, love, forgiveness, kindness, encouragement, and gratefulness. Certainly, there are so many more. How wonderful is it that you can surf them all when they are necessary? You draw in what you constantly think about; like a magnet, you will attract your thoughts. The things currently in your life are a direct result of your thoughts. When you constantly give something life in your mind, you are literally calling it into fruition. What do you want to happen? Your thoughts affect your emotions, so what you think is how you will feel. Success and failure both start in your mind, but you have the ability to choose which one you want for your life. What channel will you be on today? You are your own remote control, so set your mind now on what you want to see and the outcome you choose to live in.

Life Application:

Your life is not going to change unless you change your thinking. You have to start each day by setting your mind on the right channel for success. If you first start there, the other things will fall into place.

- Visualize right now what you want out of today? See the whole day from start to finish. Now, keep it locked on that channel. When things throughout the day seem to veer away from that channel, find a way to bring them back in line with what you see and the outcome you predicted.

- Write in your journal something you want to

happen in your life in the future. I.E.: marriage, promotion, children, and/or success for your family. See it exactly how you want it to be and make sure you give it the ending you want. Remember: God wants to give you a life of prosperity… not one of despair.

Fitness Tip:

It is time to make sure you are bringing the proper choices in the house to give your healthy, lifestyle makeover a chance to succeed. We talked about reading labels and understanding them so that you do not sabotage yourself. Now, you must go through the pantry and see what you need to get rid of and what you can replace it with.

- Go through your pantry and get rid of the Oreo cookies or the things you know are not productive to the journey you are on. It is not about depriving your self, but finding healthier alternatives.

DAY 18:

"It is Bigger than You"

"Be strong and let us fight bravely for our people and the cities of our God."

-2 Samuel 10:12 (NIV)

Life is so much bigger than your current circumstances that you think are overtaking you at the moment. It is in your response to your situations that can determine and shape you into the person you will become. Are you a fighter, a bounce-back person, a whiner, or a complainer? You are given situations to make you, but you let them break you. We have to understand that when we are going through "testing times," as we often will, we need to see where it is helping to take us to. We go through it so that we can get to it. Always take on the attitude of 'what lesson is God trying to teach me?' Ask yourself, 'how can I come out better than when I started?'

Take a moment to think about a "Team Concept" such as your family, work, school, sports teams, or an organization you are just a piece of the puzzle to, but you have people counting on you. What you do and the choices you make are not just about you; they can affect everyone else. Deciding what type of fighter you want to be, "the whiner" or "the winner," starts by understanding you are never in a fight alone. Make wise choices and when the going gets tough, you have to rise up instead of fall down and wallow in self-pity. Let the thought of representing someone other than just you and not wanting to be the weakest link, get you through. God is always with you and in every situation, and if He is in you, then He is with you. He is not going to let you fall down; the fall is always forward.

What current situation are you in right now that you know you have to step up to the plate, dig in, and be a team player? Who is counting on you? A decision you make today can affect the lives of so many for tomorrow. Talk about making a decision that will affect a team!

It was the State track meet and I was on the 4x800 team. All year, I ran the second leg. Well, the day of the STATE meet, my coach tells us he has a line-up change. I would be anchor and the anchor would be second leg. This day it was windy and I let nerves get the best of me. I thought too much instead of believing in what I have always done and my capabilities. I focused on the wrong thing and that was the change that occurred which made me change the approach of my race.

I got the baton in first with a good lead. I took off fast as if I was running a 400 which is 1 lap around instead of 2. I ran probably the fastest 400 in my 800 split ever, but I had one more lap to go. By this time I was almost a half lap ahead, but in my mind, I was frozen and scared instead of relaxed and confident. In the last stretch, I tensed up. Have you ever heard of the phrase in track, "the monkey jumped on my back"? Well, his whole ENTIRE family jumped on mine, so much that at the end, I could not feel my legs and I fell about 20 yards shy of the finish line. Remember: this is the STATE track meet. I remember seeing legs pass me by, and all I could think was, "I can't go out like this." My dad raised me to be a fighter and to not give up. I knew it was bigger than me. There were three other girls that I was representing on the relay and I also represented my entire team for the state meet. So, I crawled across the line because I could not get up. I ended up in 3rd place and didn't get disqualified because I didn't distract any of the other runners. Well, we ended up winning state by the amount of points we got for 3rd place. That was just enough to win it.

      What did I do wrong from the beginning? I thought about me more than what me being anchor would do for the team. Is there a situation, present or past, where you became self-absorbed, thinking more about how it would affect you instead of how it would help someone else? This could be something as simple as not speaking to a parent over a blow up that could affect your kids and their kids. Another example is how you handle being a single parent and what you speak about men in front of your children. These too are situations that are bigger than you! You are the example and your response can determine the outcome of the people around you that are faced with a similar situation. People are watching and if they see you make it and you are positive, more than likely, you are providing them with the power that they can over come too.

Be a fighter. It might get tough, and you might fall, but will you get up? Your response along with your attitude in it will affect others and your life forever. It can catapult you through the next battle that occurs, because you know your strength. You will be able to pull from past experiences and triumphs and see how you conquered them and know that you can do it again. Turn your trials to triumphs today. Be a team player and realize that it might not always go as planned, but you have the power within to turn it around.

Life Application:

It is important to grasp the meaning of the "team" concept. Understand that in everything we do in life, someone is watching and looking at our response. Our choices affect not just us but others as well. We can make others better.

- Write in your journal the areas in your life that others are counting on you to be successful in and how your choices directly affect them.
- Write down how you will be an asset, not a

liability, and always find ways to give your best no matter how tough it gets.

Fitness Tip:

I remember when I first started playing basketball; I had no clue what to do. What I could control was looking the part. I had on my headband, wristbands, kneepads, and my Jordans. I looked the part until I could play the part. Looking the part gets your momentum going to want to play the part well.

- Make sure you are working out in the proper attire. It is hard to want to work hard and sweat when you keep on your clothes from work.
- Get you some good workout clothes that make you feel like you are ready to take on a good workout. When you look good, you want to represent and have a good work out!

DAY 19:

"All Hail to the Queen"

"And I am convinced and sure of this very thing, that He who began a good work in you will continue until the day of Jesus Christ (right up to the time of His return), developing (that good work) and perfecting and bringing it to full completion in you."

-Philippians 1:6 (NIV)

Isn't it a relief to know that God will not give up on you even when you give up on yourself? He will continue to mold you and shape you until His perfect plan and the work He has for you is completed. I can stop there! You can jump up and down now! Thank Him that you are a work in progress. Thank Him that you are a GOOD WORK and that He is perfecting you through it all. Once you actually grasp this known fact, you will no longer beat yourself up. You understand that you are not always perfect because daily you are being perfected. In that perfection, His plan for your life is coming together to get you and make you into the beauty He has created you to be.

What do you see today when you look in the mirror? What are you calling yourself? The view you see is the same view that others see because you give them permission. Those that can't see you for who you are put you in their blind spot, so they can't see you! Pray for them! Most people are trying to figure themselves out, so them actually taking time to get to know you is impossible. This is why YOU knowing YOU is everything.

Your actions and love of yourself shows others that you are worthy and you know this confidently because God has said so. Stop downplaying your worth. It is not being cocky; it is about the connection to God's word and your belief. You are a queen. You are to be adored, loved, and favored. Isn't that what God has for you? Isn't that what He says you were created for? Walk like it and believe it in your spirit, so that naturally, it will be who you are. It is not arrogance or boasting; it is who God wants you to be: royalty. Why can't you be the queen of your castle and have the finest things? If you know that God first commands it of you, then you can demand it of yourself. Give YOU a chance! Speak to you daily that you are a queen...wonderfully and beautifully made and you are being molded daily into a beautiful piece of art.

My husband has a HUGE tattoo of "Stacie The Scorpion Queen" on his back. Before Corey Harris could SEE the Queen in me to display it, who had to see it first? I did. I had to act it, believe it, and know that it was what I deserved for myself. I am glad that he sees it... MOST DAYS! What excites me even more is NOW I see that in myself EVERYDAY, because I know that is who God molded me to be through it all. In my good and my bad days, I am still beautiful and know that you are too! No matter where you were born, what you have been through, or still might be going through, you are a QUEEN and should be adored.

No matter who has never taken the time to see it or speak it, God saw it and spoke it and you MUST too. Your approval should never have to come from man because they can never appreciate a fine piece of art like the artist himself. First, God adored you and now you should adore yourself in EVERY WAY. Close your eyes now and say out loud, "I love me some me" and really mean it.

Look in the mirror now and start calling out all the uniqueness that makes you who you are and defines and separates you from the rest! Love your curves, the shape of your lips, the color of your skin, and the wisdom in your eyes. What you need to work on, work on it, but love yourself in spite of. A man should not define you; he should just remind you! "All Hail to the Queen"! Approve yourself today; don't wait on man to approve you. The best man already has. Thank you Lord!

Life Application:

Take a bow, you queen! Give yourself permission to be valued and loved. Honestly, let go of why you are not feeling worthy anymore! Today is a brand new day for you to walk in the palace and enjoy the luxurious life that God says you are

destined for. Let Him complete you, and stop cutting yourself short of your blessings.
- Write what you will no longer accept for your life anymore, including the negative views and opinions you accepted for your life.
- Write: "I am worthy of Royalty all the days of my life! All Hail to the Queen (Your name)!"

Fitness Tip:

We talked about dressing the part now we need to make sure you complete it with your shoes. Not having the proper shoes to cross train or run in can cause back problems, shin splints, and so much more to develop and totally throw you off your journey.

- Invest in a good pair of shoes today…especially for cross training. If you are a runner, make sure you have good support. Take care of your feet and this will help to take care of your body.

DAY 20:

"Stop Looking in the Rear View Mirror"

"Jesus replied, "No one who puts his hand to the plow and looks back is fit for service in the kingdom of God."

-Luke 9:62 (NIV)

God says it so clearly that when you look back, you are not fit to move forward in the kingdom of God. The work that He has for you will never be accomplished by continually re-living in the "what was", and not living in what He has for you now. You take yourself right back to the pain, hurt, and disappointment by continuing to rehash it over and over. Let it go and move forward.

When letting go of your past or something you need to remove yourself from, think of it as embracing flying over bracing for a fall. If there is anything you need to release your hand from, do it now so that you can begin to fly to the places God has next on your itinerary. Don't let holding on continue to poison your future steps and flight. Whether it is in a relational, financial, professional, or familial issue, we have had some issues that seem like we would never get past, but we did!

Once you have finally gotten your breakthrough and you get past it, there comes a moment when something or someone might remind you of it, but don't go right back and re-live it all over again. By doing so, you are back living as if it is currently happening again and it could have been days, months, or years ago. Stop in your tracks the next time you even feel yourself riding back down memory lane and looking back. Time is fleeting and healing takes time; do not waste it on opening up a healed wound. Your emotions follow your mind, so choose to stay emotionally forward in your life.

God wants you to experience His goodness and He gives us grace, daily, to continually get it right by allowing us to move on. Don't re-live your past hurts, despair, losses, bad choices, and guilt. Learn, grow, and then blossom from them. God never said pain, hurts, and losses would not happen, but He said He would see you through and He gave you the ability to get past them. He already carried your burdens.

It is time to keep on pushing forward to your next destination. Constantly putting it in reverse is slowing down the work that you have to do and the blessings that God has waiting on you right up the road. You will not get there going in reverse. Time to push the pedal to the metal honey and drive!

Life Application:

It is so important to realize where you are headed in life and that only forward progress will get you there. We have all wasted time re-hashing or trying to make sure we are OVER IT! Tell yourself right now it is done and it is time to move on.
- Write in your journal the destination you are headed to. What are you working towards and moving forward on daily?
- Decide today that you are done putting it in reverse and that you only have the drive gear in your life from this day forward.

Fitness Tip:

It is important to make sure you are not letting too much time lapse in between meals so that your body does not think you are starving it. You shouldn't go more than three hours without eating. This is the optimum interval for ensuring that you are maintaining stable blood sugar levels that will discourage you from feeling hungry. It will also prevent your body from tapping into lean muscle for additional energy. Aim for five to six small meals per day, and make breakfast the largest of them all.
- Set a timer if you need to on your watch or phone to make sure you are feeding your body properly.
- Write the times down in your journal.

DAY 21:

"The Proverbs 31 Woman"

"Charm is deceptive, and beauty is fleeting; but a woman who fears the Lord is to be praised."

-Proverbs 31:30 (NIV)

As women, we put a lot of emphasis on our outward appearance and the works that define us. Many of us have been crippled mentally. This keeps us trapped and deceived, because we do not feel pretty enough, or our past makes us feel ugly or unworthy. We have it all wrong. The key to her beauty is a beautiful character and her spiritual life. She is a Godly woman that fears that Lord. She is a wife of noble character.

I tend to read this scripture over and over again to make sure I am keeping my life in the right perspective because who I am and should be is all in here. It defines who she is as a person, a wife, and a mother. She is called blessed by her children, and her husband, he praises her. Doesn't that sound like what we want as mothers and wives? We want to be a blessing and to have a little praise once in a while…it feels good.

What resonated in my spirit is that 'she rises early when it is still dark.' I have incorporated this into my own life by getting up at 3:30 or 4:00 am and getting an early start to my day. I get up and pray over each person including the dog in my house. Ladies: we are the strength of our families. When we rise early and bless the home, we prepare the day for our family. We cover the blessings and the promises spoken over our household, and it starts by rising early, praying, and securing our homes to win the battle. I love how it says, "She can laugh at the days to come". I love it. She can laugh because she knows the power of her God and she knows the prayers and the work she has put in to bless her family. She is secure with her works, herself, and her God. She knows that she is praised, that beauty is fleeting, and that her love of the Lord is her strength and will bring her and her house joy all days of their lives.

Make a choice to understand that your beauty is not in your appearance, but in your praise. When you can praise, you can also laugh because you have a God that will always turn your ashes into beauty! Laugh out loud!

Life Application:

It is time to see who you are as a 'Proverbs 31 Woman.' If you are waiting on blessings and your house to get in order, know that God is waiting on you. Take the focus off of the beauty on the outside and look to your character, your strength, and your wisdom, which is your beauty on the inside. Gain your strength and take control by rising early to pray and bless your family and prepare your house. When you decide to rise, so will your family. God sees you and He will richly reward you.

- Rise early when it is still dark and pray over your house and everyone in it.
- Speak blessings and their gifts individually into existence. Give them permission to succeed, and cover them with angels of protection, and allow God's grace and mercy to see them through their daily missions.
- Cook a good breakfast for you and your family. It is the most important meal, and it starts the day off right. You are feeding the spirit in preparation to go out and fulfill the promises of the day.

Fitness Tip:

Why do you eat? Your answer may be, "because I like to," but you have to get a clear understanding that eating is like gasoline for the car. It is the fuel you need to be able to operate properly. You must understand that every meal is not about the taste, but it is more about properly fueling your body. Once you understand this, making great choices will become easier.

- Start your day with eggs that are the best protein source on the planet. They contain all nine essential amino acids.

DAY 22:

"You Are Not a Knock Off"

"Make a careful exploration of who you are and the work that you have been given, and then sink yourself into that. Don't be impressed with yourself. Don't compare yourself to others. Each of you must take responsibility for doing the creative best you can with your own life."

-Galatians 6:4-5 (NIV)

    You were not created to mimic anyone else. You were created specifically to be you and to carry out the work that God has set aside for you to do. God says, in his word, not to compare you or your talents with that of another. Each and every one of us possesses distinct qualities, abilities, and creative minds to carry out our destiny. Your talents, gifts, and plans might look similar, but they are your own and you are meant to bring your own style to it. So often we try to continue on with the way things have been done because they have worked or that is what people have responded to in the past. Have you thought that God gave you something different and a new flavor to add to what has been seen as the norm? People are waiting and are in need of something different! Dare to be different and original. God did not make man as clones; he made varieties! Be secure in who He made you to be and that He gave you exactly what you needed to bring it about.

I put writing and speaking down for over a year, because I was comparing myself to other people and their success. I did not think I had enough titles behind my name. Finally, I fasted and God showed me clearly that He gave me a life of plenty to share and bless others with. My heart, my love, and my purpose were the titles that I needed. Exactly who I am as a person, a speaker, a motivator, and writer is enough for the plan He has for me to do and for the people He wants me to bless. What a relief! I no longer walk around demeaning and minimizing myself while lifting up everyone else. I embrace my own journey and uniqueness to carry it forth. I am clear in persevering in my purpose now. I know that it is BIGGER THAN ME!

Seek out a mentor and learn from people who have been successful in your craft. They will help keep you from some of the struggles you might have endured if you did not have them to guide you. Let them enlighten you and help you to stir up your gifts inside of you, so you can be encouraged. It is important to make sure the friends in your life help drive you and not down you. Many times, someone closest to you can see greatness in you before you can recognize it in yourself. These are people God has connected you with to help motivate you to keep going and to arrive at your destination. You are not looking for their approval; God is showing you that if they can believe in you, YOU should believe in you too.

Life Application:

Choose to be happy with who you are and what gifts and talents you have been blessed with. Tell yourself that they are exactly what you need and you are enough for what you want to do with your life. God has constructed you as a masterpiece with all of the necessary bells and whistles.

- Write in your journal what you think your life's mission is.
- Write down the gifts and talents you have and how they will be attributed to your journey.
- Study someone that is doing what you want to do and see what makes them a success. Think about how you can bring something unique and different to what you will be doing.

Fitness Tip:

Eating a variety of organic and unprocessed vegetables can do wonders for your health, but choosing super-nutritious kale on a regular basis may provide significant health benefits. These benefits include cancer protection and lowered cholesterol.

- Kale is the powerhouse of vegetables and known as a super green.
- There are great benefits to eating kale. Some people do not prefer it over the other greens because of its bitter taste, but try to remember that the great benefit is why you need it in your diet.

- These are the top 6 benefits of eating Kale:
    1. Detoxification and weight loss
    2. Strengthens your immune system
    3. Healthier hair, skin, and nails
    4. See clearly and stand strong
    5. Anti-inflammatory
    6. Disease Fighter

DAY 23:

"Who Can I Bless Today"

"A generous man will prosper; he who refreshes others will himself be refreshed."

-Proverbs 11:25 (NIV)

Every day is a day God is looking to bless you in some capacity. In the same way, He is watching to see if you are 'paying it forward.' Who are you blessing? In what ways are you looking to be a blessing to someone that needs your time, encouragement, knowledge, or talent? There are so many ways that we can bless others that we can find to fit into what is a busy life we all seem to lead. Letting someone go in front of you in the grocery line that has just a couple items while you have a basket full of groceries is a small gesture of kindness.

In our family, we have a pact that we look to do a good deed every day. I ask my kids at the end of the day what their good deed was for that day. I don't want them to do it as a chore or burden, but I want them to see the blessing in taking time out from thinking about themselves…to understand that giving a little to someone else can be a difference maker.

One of the greatest challenges of wanting to be your best and to live a life of excellence is doing it unselfishly. Not just being a giver, but doing it freely and with excitement speaks volumes. We finally begin to understand that God wants to bless us, but sometimes He will test us to see who we are looking to bless. Search daily by looking to see who may need you and how you can bless them. No matter how small the gesture, God sees it.

    A girlfriend of mine, who is a single mother and finds herself struggling from time to time, still looks to see how to be a blessing to someone else; she understands the importance of 'paying it forward'....to bless someone and believe in where you are going. She frequents Starbucks regularly, so she decided that once a month, she would pay for someone else's coffee. You never know how a gesture like this can help someone in their own walk and life challenges. It could be the day someone is questioning the power of God, He wants to use you to show that He is real. Be willing and ready to be used and a line of connection to express the love of God in someone's life.

    God is filling you up so that He can use you to fill up others. In your planting, you will reap a harvest. God always blesses a cheerful giver. As you are waiting for your dream to come to pass, go help someone else fulfill his or hers and watch what happens.

Just the other day I was in the kitchen cooking and my mom called. She was at work and asked would I talk to a client of hers about her grandson who is an aspiring actor. The first thought was, "why does my mom tell her clients that I will give them advice?" The other thought, for a moment, was, "I get paid to do this and she gives out my services for free." I kindly talked to the lady and it was a beautiful conversation that led to me saying I would love to be a blessing in anyway I could for her grandson. Even though those initial thoughts came to my mind, what took over was the thought that God was watching and looking at my reaction. I would not be in the position to help someone else if it wasn't for all the people who helped me through my process and fed my spirit with knowledge, encouragement, and free time.

In due time and when the timing is right, you will get paid for your gifts and talents...but realize when it is time to 'pay it forward' for free. You will reap the best rewards when you take your mind off of instant gratification. What was gratifying was realizing I had the ability to help someone else in an area that I was once a novice and am now a veteran in; it felt great. Thanks, Mom!

If you feel you have nothing to give, you absolutely do! Help someone else smile and prosper in life. Picking up the phone and making a call to a friend that you know needs words of encouragement can save a life. Don't worry about the time, or the advice just learn to be a good listener. God will tell you how to respond. Somebody needs what you have to share, so look to share it. When you look out for others, God will always make sure He looks out for you.

Life Application:

God wants you to be a builder of champion lives. He needs your help in the construction process. A simple compliment can build up someone's confidence and advance him or her to the next level. That could be just what they need to confirm that they can succeed in life and that God is looking out for them. Help reveal God in the hearts of others by being a person of service to others.

- Start today by looking for ways to be a blessing to others.
- Write down the talents, gifts, and the different ideas you have in wanting to be a service to others.
- Write the last time someone blessed you with something you didn't expect. It is time to pay it forward.

Fitness Tip:

Maintaining a healthy lifestyle is important, but it does not have to break your wallet in the process.

- Look for '2-for-1' deals at your local gyms. Most gyms will cut cost on two people signing up at the same time so ask your friend or spouse to join with you.
- Having the 'top of the line' gear is not necessary to fit in at the gym. Go for quality without breaking the bank by having what all the other gym rats are wearing. It is the quality of work you put in and not in the gear you buy.
- Start where you can. If joining a gym is not feasible or does not fit into your schedule, go to a local park or walk around your neighborhood. Give yourself the 'no excuses' mentality to help you succeed in your journey.

DAY 24:

"Let It Become Contagious"

"As iron sharpens iron, so one man sharpens another."

-Proverbs 27:17 (NIV)

When is the last time you looked at someone and you thought they seem to have it all together? They are prospering and happy and living in their dream. Maybe they are doing something similar to what you are aspiring to do. Instead of admiring from afar, get close and let their success become contagious. Let them sharpen you in the areas you need to grow in so that you too can be living in your dream. God needs you to get it so that you can help give it and become contagious in a good way to the next person.

When we first moved to LA, I knew nothing about the entertainment business... at least on the big Hollywood scale. I had a hope and a dream for my son and our family. I knew only one person. I figured if we were going to make it happen, we had to surround ourselves with the right people. I had to be able to make sure we were around it so that the kids and I could see it could become a reality. You can't just look at other people live it out and hope you can too. It must become so much a part of you that not being around it makes you feel uncomfortable and you feel out of place without it. Everyday visualize you living it, being it, and always living in the end result. What you see is what you can be.

A friend of mine, Sydney Davis, who had two, working daughters at the time, lived in our apartment building. Her youngest, Dee-Dee, played 'baby girl' on the "Bernie Mac Show," and her oldest, Aree, was shooting a movie entitled, "The Haunted Mansion" with Eddie Murphy. She took us on the set of both and she became contagious! We wanted it once we had a taste of it! We saw that we too could do it and what it would take to be a working actor in Hollywood. I am so grateful for her sharing her life and her experiences with us as it instilled hope and hard work with in us and blessed us in more ways than I think she realized. She sharpened me and got me ready to be a Hollywood mom, and it helped to prepare CJ for what it took be a well-known actor.

You can't just 'see it' for it to resonate; you have to be around it and put yourself in it. Let it actually rub off on you! Let it get so deep inside of you that it wants to explode out of you! Want to be contagious to someone else today. Let what you do help take them to places they only dreamed of going. You will find that when you are willing to help others, you are only setting yourself up for blessings to come down the road. Show them that your life is possible and help them obtain the life they want to achieve. Be contagious in a good way.

Life Application:

How many times have you been around someone positive or inspiring and it made you want to go out and do something great! It gets you going and fired up, right? They were contagious! Get around more people that bring out the best in you and look to be a person that helps bring out the best in others.

- Write down someone that has inspired you in the past and the positive impact they have made on your life.
- Call them, if you can, and thank them. They just might need that to 'rev' their spirits back up. We all need to be reminded of the good things we have done and the value that we bring to others.

Fitness Tip:

When you first join a gym, it can be overwhelming…especially to first time gym members or recommitting members. There are so many machines, old and new, that do the same thing that you often ask yourself, "Which of these should I use?"
- Keep it simple until you learn; take baby steps and add on as you get better.
- Start with a circuit training area that is sure

to target the whole body and get you accustomed to using all of your core muscles again.
- Most gyms offer a free session with a personal trainer when you join. Take advantage of that, so they can help you get familiar with the gym and gain confidence in your workout.

DAY 25:

"Be a Girl on Fire"

"His word is in my heart like fire, a fire shut up in my bones. I am weary of holding it in; indeed, I cannot."

-Jeremiah 20:9 (NIV)

God uses the analogy of having his word in you like fire! He wants it to boil inside of you and be so hot that you can feel it! He wants you to be a girl on fire! He doesn't want you holding your dreams in your heart or pondering on them. He wants others to feel the burn that you exude from being on fire. It's when you know your heart's desires and there is nothing or no one that can get in the way and blow out your flame.

I absolutely love Alicia Keys' song, "Girl on Fire;" it sums it up exactly what we need to be. You can be a 'Girl on Fire' even though you are experiencing the burdens of the world, because you know your strength and you know the flame is in your eyes. You can have both feet planted on the ground. They look at you and they see the flame because you are glowing so brightly! 'You are burning it down and you will not back down.'

Ladies, this is how we need to take on the world daily. Get up, put both feet on the ground, and know that you got it going on! Know that God has put the fire in you to win in life! Your feet might be on the ground, but you should almost be floating… knowing that God is carrying you daily and going to see you through to your destination! He just needs you to want it! He needs you to roll up your sleeves, put your dukes up, and be ready to fight for what you want! You might take a punch, but pop back up and put your dukes back up! It is our own selves who stop short of the destination. If we would have just given one more good push, the door would have blown off the hinges!

It is time to let your flame shine bright amongst the world. It is time for you to stop fanning the flame or blowing it out every time life happens! Let it burn continually in you, through it all, and keep moving forward when life tries to knock you backwards as it sometimes will. Make a commitment today not wallow in self-pity, and don't give in; start figuring out how to dig in.

Remember: God has a purpose and can use everything that happens to you to advance you. When everybody else is living life defeated and down, you stay alive and choose daily to get up on the inside and be happy. You are a woman of God that He has purposed and given you passion; light your flame and be on fire!

Life Application:

If you weren't on fire, you should be now! You should be dodging anything that is trying to blow your flame out! Every day, make a conscience effort to go out and be your best and be happy doing it! You know what you want, so don't stop until you get it and enjoy doing it! Hold your head up and plant both feet on the ground and start today by claiming everyday as a victory for choosing to live as a girl on fire!

- Write down what being a girl on fire means to you.
- Every day, you should journal what you did to stay encouraged and to achieve your goal of being happy.
- Cross out and write a positive thought over any negative thoughts you had.

Fitness Application:

Keeping a consistent workout schedule is important but so is taking time off to allow your body to recover. If you are feeling sore, that might just mean you are working your muscles to a new level, but you never want to over do it and let soreness turn into pulling a muscle that can set you back even further. It is important to allow time in between workouts to let your muscles repair.
- Start with a day on and a day off.
- The day after you engage in heavy training,

look to do a lighter form of conditioning like gulfing or walking. Stretching on your off days can be very effective for helping with soreness, increasing your flexibility, and helping to give you long lean muscles.

DAY 26:

"You Have the Winning Ticket"

"If you belong to Christ, then you are Abraham's seed, and heirs according to his promise."

-Galatians 3:29 (NIV)

Who do you belong to? Whose child are you? Galatians 3:29 reminds us that if you belong to Christ, you are the seed of Abraham and his heirs according to HIS PROMISE. So often we are waiting on the big ticket. Many people stand in line daily to play the lottery, buy scratch offs, and pray a certain relative might pass on soon so that they can become an heir to their inheritance. It sounds crazy, but you know it's true. They are wasting precious time investing in the wrong thing and in the wrong person! The ticket is already in their pocket as they walk around aimlessly waiting for a miracle that will probably never happen. If it by some chance does happen, they are not happy, because they put their faith in the wrong ticket.

It is important to know who has your back, and whose lineage you truly are a descendant of. You are a descendant of the most high! He has made you an heir to the same promises of Abraham! Like Abraham, you have promises that God has made to you. Like Abraham, you will go through life doubting and trying to take matters into your own hands, because the promises of God seems like they just might not come to pass. Abraham finally started to believe and have faith; when the final test came to sacrifice his son Isaac, he remembered the promise of God, so he stood and he believed. Friends: if you don't stand for something, you will fall for anything. The best investment is banking on you and what has been deposited in you. You have got to stand up and trust that God has given you the winning ticket. It is up to you to recognize it and cash it in.

Today you have to know that you are a child of God, and that He has created a great work in you. Sorrow might come, disappointments will come, fear will set in, but you know the promises of God. Life is not made to be easy, but God does want it to be good. It is time to let the good times roll honey! He wants you to succeed far beyond what you could ever imagine. Decide today to stop chasing after the wrong inheritance and live within the richness, joy, and blessings that God has promised for you. It is time to cash in! Claim your winning ticket!

Life Application:

Congratulations, you're a million dollar winner! You can walk around everyday excited knowing YOU are the winning ticket… literally. You have the inheritance of the Almighty Father that will keep you fully paid far beyond just money. With the joy, love, perseverance, gifts, blessings, and talents that you have, no millions of dollars can ever replace them. You are rich! Start today by walking in victory and passing the test of doubt, fear, and hopelessness. You are the child of the richest man on the planet and He has promised to leave you an inheritance, so a poor mentality is one less thing to ponder on! Today, ponder on how you will fulfill the richness and the greatness that you have been left with!

- Write in your journal the promises you know that God has spoken to you and that you have doubted and given up on.
- Think of the promises that you have fulfilled and write those down.
- Decide today that you are rich and highly favored and that with God, you know all things are possible.
- One-by-one, begin fulfilling the things you have lost hope in but still have on your heart to bring forward. Have faith that God's promises are true and that He will see you through. As you fulfill them, write them in your journal.

Fitness Application:

During the holiday season and family vacations, it is easy to go backwards and sabotage all your hard work. Don't get side tracked by traveling and throwing off your work out and eating regimen. It is important to remember the goals you have set before you at all times. You have worked so hard to get there, so you don't want to throw it all away on one trip or throughout the Holidays! Make your celebration last one day…in moderation and not for a whole three months straight! Consistency is the key. Here are a few tips to help you not to sabotage your hard earned work, but make sure you still get to enjoy!

- Get in your daily intake of water regardless of what you eat.
- Drink water before each meal or snack.
- Staying hydrated is the key to not overeating, avoiding retaining water, and feeling bloated.
- Always leave something on your plate to enjoy for a snack or lunch for the next day. This helps with over-eating, and guilt (HA).
- Take workout clothes even if you don't work out as much as you normally do; try to find something different to participate in that you don't normally get to enjoy at home.
- Remember what it took to get where you are and the lives you have affected other than your own. This journey is much bigger than you or the number on the scale.

Day 27:

"Follow YOUR Plan"

"For I know the plans I have for you, says the Lord, they are plans for good, not for disaster, to give you a future and a hope."

-Jeremiah 29:11 (NIV)

Just like an architect creates a blue print, so does God have a plan for your life. It is so awesome to know that when God created us, He did it, intentionally, knowing that there was a plan for each of us. You are molded to perfection and with good intentions. This is refreshing, right? How often do we look for someone else to validate the plan for our lives?

I was on a conference call the other day and the series was about calling out your greatness. Let's break that down to make it very simple: greatness is YOUR PLAN. The speaker quoted Mike Murdoch, a pastor that preaches on prosperity, by saying, "If you are not in the CENTER of your expertise, then you are in the MIDDLE of your weakness!" I love that! Either way, you are in the middle of something, so it might as well be the plan for YOUR life.

It is necessary to be surrounded by people who inspire you to be better and by those who you are constantly learning and growing from. The problem comes in when they try to tell you who you are or you let their life and their dreams become yours. Remember: you are original. Although many might do the same thing, there are no carbon copies. I like to look at what God has destined for me as the EXAMPLE, and the others that preceded me were the SAMPLE.

Don't live in confusion by constantly letting someone else put limitations on your growth. Don't let them put a lid on something so preciously put inside of you that you are ready to let out. It is important that you listen to God when it comes to doubt or any major decisions; He will always provide you with clarity. God has your future filled with faith and hope and we must seek Him as our coach to guide us through.

Being a former point guard, I am very familiar with the importance of a coach and a winning play book. This is how I talk to God most days, "Good morning coach; I am lacing up my shoes. What do you have for me today?" "How can I help the team win?" God will bring the right people, books, videos, organizations, etc. to help execute the plan and give you the confirmation you need to stay the course. Start listening to what the ultimate decorator, illustrator, coach, and craftsman has worked out just for you. Put earplugs in when the negative, demeaning, and pushy people, who are not certain of their own journey, try to lead you on yours.

Life Application:

Isn't it amazing when people know more about what is good for you than they know for themselves? I am not saying to never take advice from others, but learn to decipher what is to be used and what is to be tossed as it pertains to your plans. God will place the right people in your path to speak on His behalf. What is IMPORTANT is KNOWING your plan and then you can discern what to deposit and what to dispose of when people are in your ear. It is also clearer to see the devil in a blue dress when you are certain of the color red! Be certain of what your journey looks like and the amazing things that God has for you in it. When you entertain too many other things, distractions will put you in your weakness. Build on your strengths, and let the people God chooses help you on your journey and help you with your weakness.

- Write in your journal what your plan looks like.
- What in your plan can already be marked off?
- What in your plan still needs to be perfected?
- What are the necessary steps you need to take to carry out what you know is your blue print?
- Write down the people who have been successful at what you want to do or the

place of business that is similar to yours and let that be your sample, but follow through with you being the EXAMPLE.
- Dare to be Different!

Fitness Application:

Knowing the plan, as we see, is very crucial to living in our purpose and being our best. By now, you should know what exercises and the things that you eat that work well for your body. It is important to record what works so that you can always go back to 'old faithful.'

- Record in your journal the foods that have been working more as a medicine for you. Keep note of the foods that allow you to feel good, give you energy, and help you obtain your weight goals.
- Record the exercises that you know kick your butt but will help shape you up!

DAY 28:

"Use Your Key to Set You Free"

"It is for freedom that Christ has set us free. Stand firm, then and do not let yourselves be burdened again by a yoke of slavery."

-Galatians 5:1 (NIV)

Today, before you walk out the door, I want to make sure that you do it "Free". Far too long, we have held ourselves captive when all we had to do was use the key to set ourselves free and walk out the door a new person. We shackle ourselves to our fears, doubts, and unforgiveness way too much. We walk around tied up and held in bondage for years, not knowing why it feels like the weight of the world is upon us.

If you want to lose weight and get rid of the migraines you have been constantly having, it is time to FORGIVE and LIVE. The constant arguments, failed relationships, failed businesses, depression, loneliness, and fears need to be cuffed and you need to walk away and leave it behind you TODAY.

Say this to yourself over and over until you feel it deep inside your spirit: "I FORGIVE myself!" Say it again, "I FORGIVE _____." Really mean it and see in your mind the things that have been holding you back as if they are cut up or burned up in flames.

God says, "It is for FREEDOM that He has set YOU free, so stand firm and do not let yourselves be burdened again by the yoke of being in slavery!" You get to choose the course which is the curse or blessing. He has already set us free, yet we continue to burden ourselves AGAIN when He says not to. So the only person that can set you free now is you! He has given you the key and the promise that there is no need to worry yourself anymore. You have been forgiven so that you can live!

Each day starts a new slate, but we continue to write over things that are still there and think we can read them. No! That is a MESS. It becomes confusion, cluttered, and it stops making sense. Clean your slate!

Erase what was and start with what should be TODAY. No more replaying the mistakes of your past and keeping them on the screen of your heart. It is time for you to start living the life you deserve and that will only happen when you stop being defined and tied to your past. The past is to pass through so that you can get to the destiny that God has set forth for you to live FREELY IN. You have the key, so use it today to set yourself free and walk into the promises that God has for your life. Forgive so that you can live. Practice discipline and condition yourself daily, mentally and spiritually, so you will be ready when game time comes!

Life Application:

You might be in tears or you might be jumping for joy right now! You are no longer enslaved to your past failures and mistakes. You have wiped your slate clean and you are ready to write something new and legible for your life to begin.

- In RED or BOLD, write in your journal the current date and the phrase, "I AM FREE."
- As I stated earlier, set yourself free by forgiving yourself, whoever it is you need to forgive, and maybe a few specific things you need to get over. Write them down on a piece of paper.
- Pin it up on a board as if it is pinned to the cross and state over it, one-by-one, "I am free of…"
- Now burn it or throw it away and know that it has been nailed to the cross as our Lord and Savior was and see that the board is clean and ready to be used in a new way! Let God use you in a new way today.

Fitness Application:

Since we are talking about starting with a clean slate and forgiveness, we need to do the same thing when it comes to body transformation and health. It is time to let go of those bad eating habits, procrastination, and excuses for the time you do not have and the genes you were not given. Knowledge and opportunity, to which we have all been privy to, is the key to unlocking your best in your health and fitness goals. No more looking at where you are or what you have failed to do in the past; look at where you are going to and see yourself as you will be. If you keep looking at yourself where you are now and not at your progression, you will remain there. Celebrate the baby steps and your commitment towards a lifestyle change. Look ahead and imagine where you can go…not looking back is the key. Discover the possibilities, first in your mind and your body, and health will follow.

- Write down the old habits and things that have failed you in the past when it comes to working out and eating.
- Pin them to the board and say, "This is no longer who I am."
- Throw them away or burn them and know that your old ways are GONE.
- Pin your new eating and workout regimen, for you to see daily, to the board. Likewise pin your goals and what you have achieved so far.
- Claim today that you are victorious and you are living in a new way of health and fitness that is successful and you are now an example to others of what is achievable.

DAY 29:

"Do Me a Favor"

"Ask and it will be given to you; seek and you will find; knock and the door will be opened to you."

-Matthew 7:7 (NIV)

I remember my mom clearly saying to me, when I was growing up, "A closed mouth won't get fed." She would always say, "Speak up Stacie; what do you want? I can't read your mind." This was one of the best things my mother could have ingrained in me. She was teaching me to ASK and to do it LOUD and PROUD. If you don't ask, someone else will! Don't let your blessing or your desires go to waste just because you didn't ask. In God's word, HE says to ASK. Not only does He say to ask and seek it, but He says it CAN and WILL be yours! It is a spoken guarantee. God wants your life to be one that you are proud to have and excited to exist in. He does not want us down and out.

Too often, we ask the wrong people for a favor or look to the wrong people for help. The best help lives within. It is time for you to live "favor minded." Know that God is in the blessing business on a REGULAR BASIS! He is waiting for you to say, loud and proud, the things you want Him to do. He has so many awesome things He wishes for you, but He understands the importance of wanting it for yourself. By opening your mouth, you are releasing your faith and bringing home your blessing!

I pray blessings of favor over my family daily. Even for something as simple as getting the best parking spot, being able to get something that others can't find and say is no longer available, or being picked as a long shot for something, I declare God's favor as I know He is willing and that I am worthy of it! All you have to do is ask, believe, and be willing to receive. When you live favor minded, people will do things for you and they have no clue why they were led to do it. Start each day favor minded and feeling blessed and you will consistently attract that to you!

If you continue going through life doubting or not feeling worthy, you are cutting off the blessings that has prepared for you even before they can get to you. Line up with your life by knowing you are first worthy and believing that God has great things in store for you. YOU have to be expectant and ask for the blessings to flow. Let Him know, today, that you are ready and that you believe in him and that He can count on you.

My neighbor told me that she received a free car. Then my kids told me their dad received a free Mercedes truck from a friend! Ok! So I knew God was in the blessing business as it was all around me. So I decided to ask God for a favor. "Lord, can you give me a free car?" At this time, I had a very busy teenager, so another car was necessary. This is a true story. I consumed myself with it and spoke it over my life believing it would happen. I told you it is not for us to worry about the how, but to be prepared for the when.

My dad mentioned if he could find a specific car, color, and price, he would buy it and give me his truck. Daddy had no idea that I was praying for a free car. We looked for the car he wanted and it was either: not the price, not the color, and/or the car was miles away and would have to be shipped. Then out of the blue, he decided to look in the newspaper which he never does. There was someone selling the car he wanted with the color he wanted and lived only 10 miles away! We were both amazed that we spoke it and God allowed it to come right in his own town! The man that was selling the car remembered him from work! They actually worked together at General Motors! Daddy bought the car he dreamed of having and I got a free car that we bought him years ago. The car is in great shape, it reminds me of my daddy, and it was FREE!! God showed me the power of putting your mind on the things you want and literally speaking and claiming them! God even went above and beyond that and my mom ended up getting a new car and blessed my son with her older Lexus! So, God is into blessing you above and beyond! We received not just 1, but 2 free cars!

Ask, seek, knock, and the door will be opened. Believe today when God says He is in the blessing business! He wants you to have all of the desires of your heart, but you need to speak up so that He knows you believe that you can receive them. What is it that you want? What is it that drives you? It is not only possible, but it is necessary for you to live the fruitful life that you are meant to have. Declare favor over your life and live in your abundance daily.

Life Application:

It really is as simple as asking, but you have to also release the faith within to know that what you ask for is possible. One touch of God's favor can change your life forever! Today, you must choose to trust that He has your best interest at heart. You are a VIP, so see yourself as worthy of having the best. Start expecting the favor of God to show up in your life.

- Think of times that you have received something unexpectedly or you were shocked by an outcome that worked out in YOUR FAVOR.
- Write these things that come to mind down in your journal.
- Write down some things that are approaching for you and that you know you need the favor of God to help you see it through.
- Speak those things into existence declaring

that God does not want you to be the long shot; He wants you to be the winning shot!

Fitness Application:

Do yourself a favor and make your health and fitness lifestyle count. A few ways to make it count is by staying proactive daily and looking for ways to enhance what you are doing daily. Take time out today to see how you can better your eating at each meal and take your workout to the next level.

- Look to cut back on calories at each meal by going lower in fat content, portions, and making healthier substitutions.
- There are ways to make your meals or treats taste better without all the heavy fat content. Your taste buds will adjust and you will feel most gratified because you know you ate sensibly.
- How many calories you are burning during your workouts does not always matter if you aren't feeling like you put in some work. Switch up your workout with higher intensity and more challenging exercises now to take you to your next level of change. Heavier weights and shorter burst of sprinting followed by shorter recovery will help to challenge you and take your results to the next level.

DAY 30:

"Advance Your Second Chances"

"As for you, you meant evil against me, but God meant it for good in order to bring about this present result, to preserve many people alive."

-Genesis 50:20 (NIV)

In life, there will be disappointments, maybe even a surprise ending, but all of it is pertinent for the road that God is preparing for you ahead. Your adversities are to advance you. In the BLESSINGS and the TESTINGS of our Lord and Savior, there are no exceptions. He loves you enough to allow you to go through, so you can get to His perfect plan for your life. He is a forward thinking God. God is always steps ahead. He is always guiding you and leading you in the direction of the REAL victory. We get so stuck on being the victim that we stop short of the victory. With everything so quick at our fingertips considering microwaves, DVRs, and fast food lines, we want everything right now. The best food is the food that has been slowly cooked, and the best ideas and inventions sometimes take years. Be willing to see the end result but also be able to enjoy the journey and know that learning and growing is important. God is always looking to take you higher and to give you hope and a prosperous future.

Whether it is a failed marriage, opportunity at work you wanted, you bombed a test, or you simply missed out by not being ready or messed up, remember that God always presents another opportunity. He knew before the outcome came, what you would do. So no more beating yourself up about blowing it. We all BLOW IT, and guess what, you might BLOW IT again. It is in your response that progress happens and when we are able to figure out the answer to the important question, "where do I go from here?"

Don't stay down; decide how you will get back up and get back on course. Take advantage of the second, third, and fourth chances that await you to be able to correct and redirect your future. It is NEVER too late for a new career choice, getting in shape, finding true love, forgiving, or reconnecting with family and loved ones. Every day is a new day to start over, but it is a choice you must make daily.

In reading this book, I know there have been so many emotions you have connected with: new found excitement, hope, determination, joy, forgiveness, and then there comes fear and doubt. There is that voice, just as we get excited, that wants to tear us down and reminds us of all the wrong choices, decisions, and mistakes we have made in the past that ask, "why do you think you can do it now?"

Speak to that voice every time it wants to rise up by saying that it no longer has reign over your thoughts and your life! That power belongs to God who created you and wants you to experience every good thing He has for you. Get rid of all your dream killers, and stealers in your life. Surround yourself with the "go getters", and the "do betters". If you fall, get up and do it again. If it fails, try it again until you get it right. If you want it, you can have it, and if you can think it, you can do it!

What is it that needs a second chance in your life? Take advantage of learning and starting a new day fresh and whole again. Look to advance every second chance!

Life Application:

Are you ready to take advantage of the never-ending opportunities that God has for you? Just because one thing didn't have the ending you wanted, does not mean it is the end. God will turn things around that seem sour and make them sweet. So sweet He will make them that you will experience a cavity! When you know that He means no harm to come to you but only good to be the result, claim "Oh, okay God; I know you are up to something. You have something better in the works." Watch how that shift in your attitude will show you the positive shift that He is wanting to take place in your life.

- Write down something you have been disappointed about or something that truly devastated you?
- How did you respond?
- How would you respond now if that were to happen to you?
- What are some of the things you know you need to advance on your second chance and be grateful about?

Fitness Application:

Investing in your overall health in wellness is a must for life, longevity, and happiness. Having your journal for your meals and workouts help to keep you on track and compiles a database for you to always be able to refer to. Having things readily available and accessible will help you to stay on track and keep it simple yet effective.

- Start looking for restaurants that you like, even new ones, and put together the meals that will keep you on track.
- Go online for the menus or grab them when you are out.
- The more you already know about a restaurant, the more it will prevent you from choosing something on a whim and sabotaging your plan.
- Planning ahead eliminates guessing and it is the key to your success.

DAY 31:

"IM-POSSIBLE"

"I can do all things through Christ who strengthens me."

-Philippians 4:13 (NIV)

Yes! Yes you can! Everything in you and about you is possible! After filling your mind and body, daily, with what God says about you and writing down how it applies to your life, you are ready! The scripture above is one that most people know and can quote easily but fail to live by daily and adhere to what it says! YOU can do all things because God has supplied you with the necessary STRENGTH. We have read in past days about courage, love, talents, gifts, and blessings that He has bestowed upon us, but the most important thing to leave you with is that you do have the muscles to see it through. Your mind, your heart, and your physical body are muscles that you can train daily and shape them into what you need them to be to perform at your best.

I want you to take a deep breath and gather your thoughts on what these last 31 days have done for you mentally and spiritually. Look at the growth, the happiness, and the peace that has taken place. You have learned how to adjust through a bad moment and not make it a bad memory that could last forever. Live and let go so that you can keep striving to achieve the abundance that God wants you to have. Be disciplined and be diligent about the life you want to have for you and your family. See your outcome always as victorious so that when you are going through it, you know that in the end, you will still win. You are on the winning team when you believe in you and you know the God that is in you.

Every day that you wake up is a new day for you to recharge and make YOU happen. If there is not chalk around you, then that means you are up and alive and the only thing that gets crossed off is another mark towards your goal. Take a stand today for YOU, or fall today for anything. Take time to appreciate you and acknowledge what you have come through and where you are capable of going. Always count you 'in' and not 'out!' It is important to fill your spirit daily with things that will help program your mind in the right direction and line it up with the life you want to lead. What you are reading is what you are becoming. What you are watching on TV becomes your reality.

You will always have a choice, so choose wisely. Choose to love you, be you, and do you to the best of your ability. What you can't do, God can do. Be willing to always do your part and let Him do His. The person that you are is no mistake. Everything that you have been through is no mistake. There are different routes to get to the same destination, but you will get there.

In the hard times, stick and stay positive claiming that God has paved a way, even when the clouds are gray and the sun is not shining. Be a light for you and help continue to shine it so that others will also see that they too are possible. Live daily knowing that Impossible is nothing, but I'M-Possible is everything.

Life Application:

You are POSSIBLE! Isn't that great? Realizing that everything we have been through is to help mold us into the great piece of work that we are to become. You are capable of being the author of your own story and the decorator of your own house. Continue to seek God daily to start your day and fill you up so that you don't start on empty. Fill up so you can lift 'you' up before anybody else tries to bring you down. You need to be up so high that they are not able to reach you. Put on your armor, and be ready to fight for YOU.

- Remember the questions I asked at the very beginning? Go back and re-write your answers.
- Hopefully, the questions that you could not answer are clear to you now.
- Post your final answers on your mirror and let it be a daily reminder of who you are and the life you want to live. See that you are POSSIBLE in everyway!
- Pay it forward and if this book has blessed you, refer it to someone else or bless someone else with a book to help them to also discover their possibilities.

Fitness Application:

How do you feel? It has been a whole month of making small changes with a BIG difference for your life. Take some measurements and get on the scale to see how much lighter you are. Remember not to always depend on the scale, because muscle weighs more than fat. Inches and the way your clothes are fitting are the best way to tell of your progress.

- Congratulate yourself for the changes you have made and treat yourself to a leisure walk to smell the roses, or do something you enjoy; go dancing!
- Look to make adjustments in your eating and workouts. You don't want to plateau.
- Get a new book, or join a workout group online to learn new ideas; stay connected to people who are also on this journey with you.
- Look to be inspired and find someone to inspire.

Book Reviews

By: Tracie Bonds

But first, be concerned about his kingdom and what has his approval. Then all these things will be provided for you.

- *Matthew 6:33 GOD'S WORD Translation (GW)*

    I've known Stacie since our sons played little league together over 10 years ago. She's the most loyal person I know. Her passion for life, success, and ability to lead others to live their dreams pours out of her in every conversation. She's a player/coach at heart…always growing herself so she can help others grow.

    In this book, Stacie's done an excellent job of laying everything out for you in the right order. This is all in an effort for you to obtain success in all areas of your life. Follow along, daily, by doing the work that she suggests, in the proper order, and I am confident you will experience a life transformation.

Tracie Bonds

-Life & Business Coach, Entrepreneur, Author, Speaker, Founder: Pro31 Biblical Business Training

Stacie has truly been a blessing in my life. We met in 1995 in Houston, TX. At our very first meeting, God made her my protector, teacher, confidant, trainer, friend, and auntie to my kids.
She was and is my angel on earth. I can count on one hand the times I've really seen her sad. It isn't that she doesn't get sad or feel despair, but she comes back swinging…wiser and better than ever.

Her energy and spirit is contagious to those around her. This book is a testimony of her spirit, drive, determination, and life. I'm so proud of you my dear friend and may God continue to bless you abundantly!

Mechelle McNair
- Former NFL Wife, RN

My mom has been my biggest inspiration. She has instilled in me the will to win in every area of my life. This book is our journey and I pray it will bless you and that her leadership will guide you into your "Greatness" as she has done and continues to do in our home.

CJ Sanders
- Actor best known as the "Young Ray," All American Football and Track Athlete

Made in the USA
Charleston, SC
19 November 2013